Mazes Galore!

David E. McAdams

Copyright 2025 Life is a Story Problem LLC. All rights reserved. No part of this book may be copied, stored, or transmitted by any means without express written consent of the copyright holder.

Other Books by David E. McAdams

Parrot Colors, Flower Colors, Space Colors, People Colors, Royal Colors – Introduces the concept of colors using beautiful images. For ages 0-6.

The Dragon Number Book, The Elvish Number Book, The Fairy Number Book, Red Neck Number Book, The Unicorn Number Book, The Truck Number Book – Enjoy learning the numbers 0-10 with amazing and fun images. Great for ages 2-6.

Numbers Coloring Book, Dragon Numbers Coloring Book, Animal Numbers Coloring Book and **Geometric Shapes Coloring Book** – Provide hours of fun with themed coloring pages while teaching the basics of math.

Amazing Numbers – Learn to compare number values to solve a maze.

If I Had a Monster – A charming story where monsters represent important people in a child's life. Fun for all ages.

Even Generals Take Out the Garbage – A heartwarming story that teaches children the importance of doing chores. Suitable for young readers.

Shapes – A playful introduction to geometric shapes, designed for children aged 3-6.

Geometric Nets Project Book – Contains 80 geometric nets to copy, cut out, and assemble into 3D polyhedra. Ideal for ages 9 and up.

Geometric Nets Mega Project Book – Features 253 geometric nets to copy, cut out, and construct into 3D polyhedra. Suitable for ages 9 and up.

Numbers – A beginner-friendly book introducing the concept of numbers. Recommended for ages 5-7.

What is Bigger Than Anything? (Infinity) – A fascinating look at the concept of infinity for curious minds aged 6-8.

Swing Sets (Set Theory) – A comprehensive introduction to set theory, tailored for students aged 7-10.

One Penny, Two – Join Jerry on his journey to buy a sports car as his penny doubles each day. A captivating read for ages 8-12.

Learning With Play Money Activity Kit – A fun hands-on kit to teach counting and large numbers with over $2,000,000 in play money. Best for ages 8-12.

My Favorite Fractals (Volumes 1 & 2) – A visual treat of high-resolution fractal images, appealing to all ages.

50 Riddles – A beautifully illustrated book of 50 new riddles.

All Math Words Dictionary – A comprehensive math dictionary covering key concepts in pre-algebra, algebra, geometry, and pre-calculus.

The First Million Digits of Pi, The First Million Digits of e, The Square Root of 2 to One Million Digits, The First Hundred Thousand Prime Numbers – A fun celebration of math constants, suitable for all ages.

For an up-to-date list of books, visit https://www.DEMcAdams.com.

Table of Contents

How to Solve a Maze: A Practical Guide...1
   1. The Wall-Following Rule (Right-Hand or Left-Hand Rule).............................1
   2. Look Ahead and Plan...1
   3. Work Backward from the Exit...1
   4. Use a Pencil Lightly (for Paper Mazes)...2
   5. Leave Breadcrumbs (Physical Mazes)...2
   6. Dead-End Filling (Algorithmic Approach)...2
   7. Map It Out (For Complex Mazes)...3
   Bonus Tips...3
9×12 Easy Square Mazes...4
12×15 Easy Square Mazes...9
12×15 Medium Square Mazes...14
20×24 Medium Square Mazes...19
20×24 Hard Square Mazes...24
30×37 Hard Square Mazes...29
9×12 Easy Triangular Mazes...34
12×15 Easy Triangular Mazes...39
12×15 Medium Triangular Mazes..44
20×24 Medium Triangular Mazes..49
20×24 Hard Triangular Mazes..54
30×37 Hard Triangular Mazes..59
12×19 Easy Hexagonal Mazes...64
15×23 Easy Hexagonal Mazes...69
15×23 Medium Hexagonal Mazes..74
24×39 Medium Hexagonal Mazes..79
24×39 Hard Hexagonal Mazes..84
37×59 Hard Hexagonal Mazes..89
9×12 Easy Diamond Mazes..94
12×15 Easy Diamond Mazes..99
12×15 Medium Diamond Mazes..104
20×24 Medium Diamond Mazes..109
20×24 Hard Diamond Mazes..114
30×37 Hard Diamond Mazes..119
9×12 Easy Snub Square Mazes..124
12×15 Easy Snub Square Mazes..129
12×15 Medium Snub Square Mazes..134
20×24 Medium Snub Square Mazes..139
20×24 Hard Snub Square Mazes..144
30×37 Hard Snub Square Mazes..149

9×12 Easy Snub Square 2 Mazes..154
9×12 Easy Cairo Mazes...159
12×15 Easy Cairo Mazes...164
13×16 Easy Cairo Mazes...169
13×15 Medium Cairo Mazes...174
20×24 Medium Cairo Mazes...179
20×24 Hard Cairo Mazes...184
30×37 Hard Cairo Mazes...189
20×20 Hard Circular Mazes..194
25×25 Hard Circular Mazes..199
30×30 Hard Circular Mazes..204
35×35 Hard Circular Mazes..209
9×12 Easy Square Triangle Mazes..215
12×15 Easy Square Triangle Mazes..220
12×15 Medium Square Triangle Mazes..225
20×24 Medium Square Triangle Mazes..230
20×24 Hard Square Triangle Mazes..235
30×37 Hard Square Triangle Mazes..240
Solutions..245

How to Solve a Maze: A Practical Guide

Mazes are puzzles made of paths and dead ends. Whether you're working on paper, navigating a hedge maze, or solving a digital labyrinth, the goal is the same: find the path from the entrance to the exit. Here are several effective strategies you can use:

1. The Wall-Following Rule (Right-Hand or Left-Hand Rule)

How it works:

Place one hand (right or left) on a wall at the entrance.

Keep that hand in contact with the wall as you walk.

Follow the wall continuously, turning whenever the wall does.

When to use:

Works best in simply connected mazes (no isolated sections).

May not work in mazes with islands or floating walls (sections not connected to the outer walls).

Pros: Easy to follow; doesn't require memory or mapping.

Cons: Can take a long time if the correct path is far from the outer wall.

2. Look Ahead and Plan

How it works:

Before moving, scan ahead for possible dead ends or shorter paths.

Use visual clues to anticipate which paths loop back or lead forward.

When to use:

Useful for paper mazes or mazes with good visibility.

Pros: Can avoid backtracking and speed up progress.

Cons: Requires careful observation and sometimes trial and error.

3. Work Backward from the Exit

How it works:

Start at the exit and trace the path backward to the start.

This can make identifying the correct path easier.

When to use:

Only possible if you can see the entire maze.

Pros: Sometimes the exit side has fewer options, making it easier to trace.

Cons: Not always allowed or visible in physical mazes.

4. Use a Pencil Lightly (for Paper Mazes)

How it works:

Lightly trace your path in pencil so you can erase wrong turns.

Mark dead ends to avoid returning to them.

When to use:

Great for printed or drawn mazes.

Pros: Helps keep track of explored paths.

Cons: Needs patience and focus.

5. Leave Breadcrumbs (Physical Mazes)

How it works:

Drop a small marker (like a coin or rock) at intersections.

Mark paths you've tried to avoid going in circles.

When to use:

For real-life maze experiences, like corn mazes or escape rooms.

Pros: Helps avoid retracing.

Cons: Not always permitted or possible.

6. Dead-End Filling (Algorithmic Approach)

How it works:

Identify and mark all dead ends.

Work backward, eliminating paths that lead nowhere.

When to use:

On paper or digital mazes where full layout is visible.

Pros: Guarantees you isolate the correct path.

Cons: Can be time-consuming for large mazes.

7. Map It Out (For Complex Mazes)

How it works:

Draw a map of paths you've explored.

Mark branches, loops, and intersections.

When to use:

Complex mazes with many loops or when solving over time.

Pros: Creates a record; very effective.

Cons: Requires time and effort.

Bonus Tips

Stay Calm: Getting lost is part of the experience.

Use Landmarks: In real mazes, look for unique features.

Track Your Choices: Mentally or physically note left/right turns.

Know the Goal: Is the goal the center, an exit, or a hidden object?

9×12 Easy Square Mazes

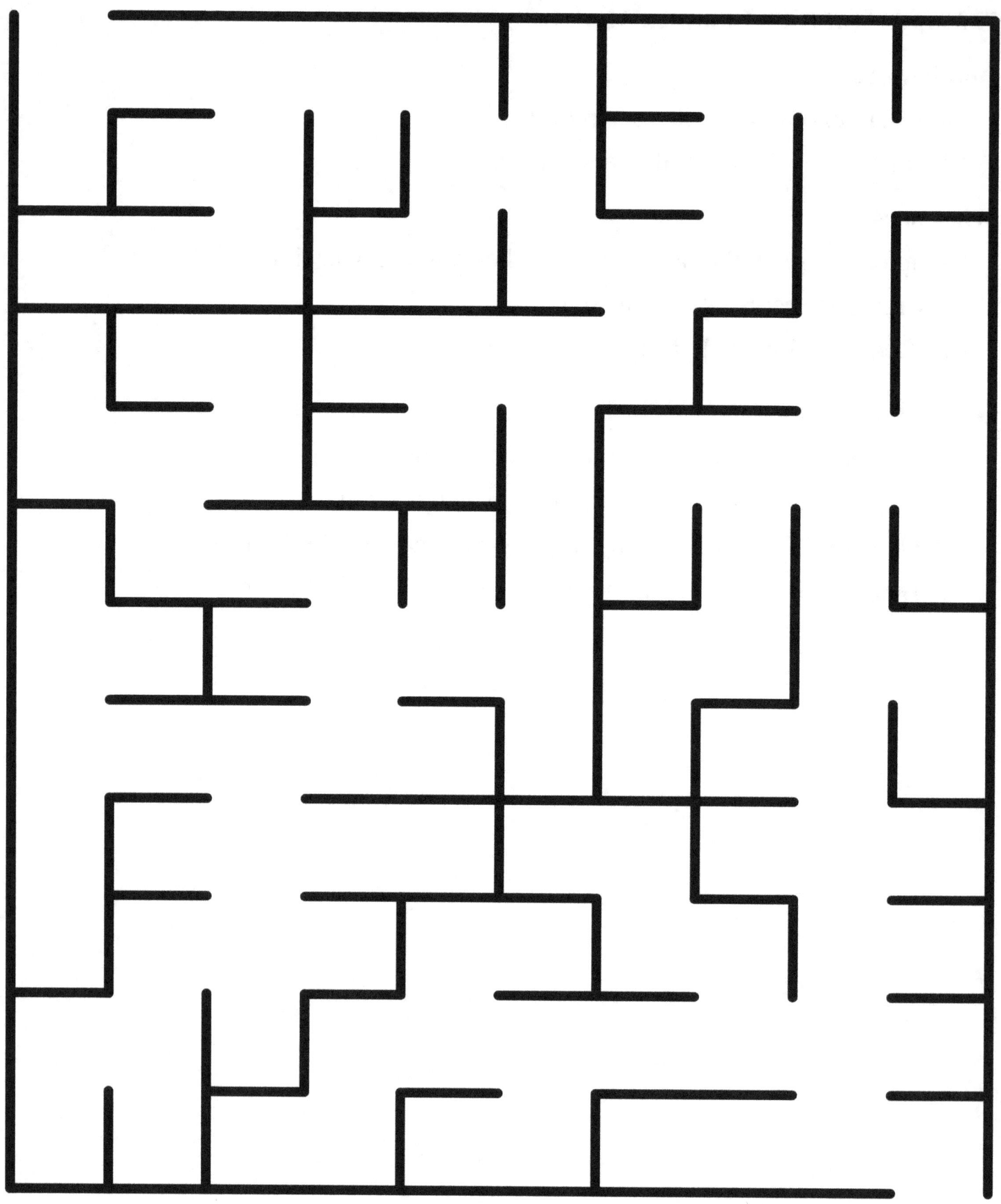

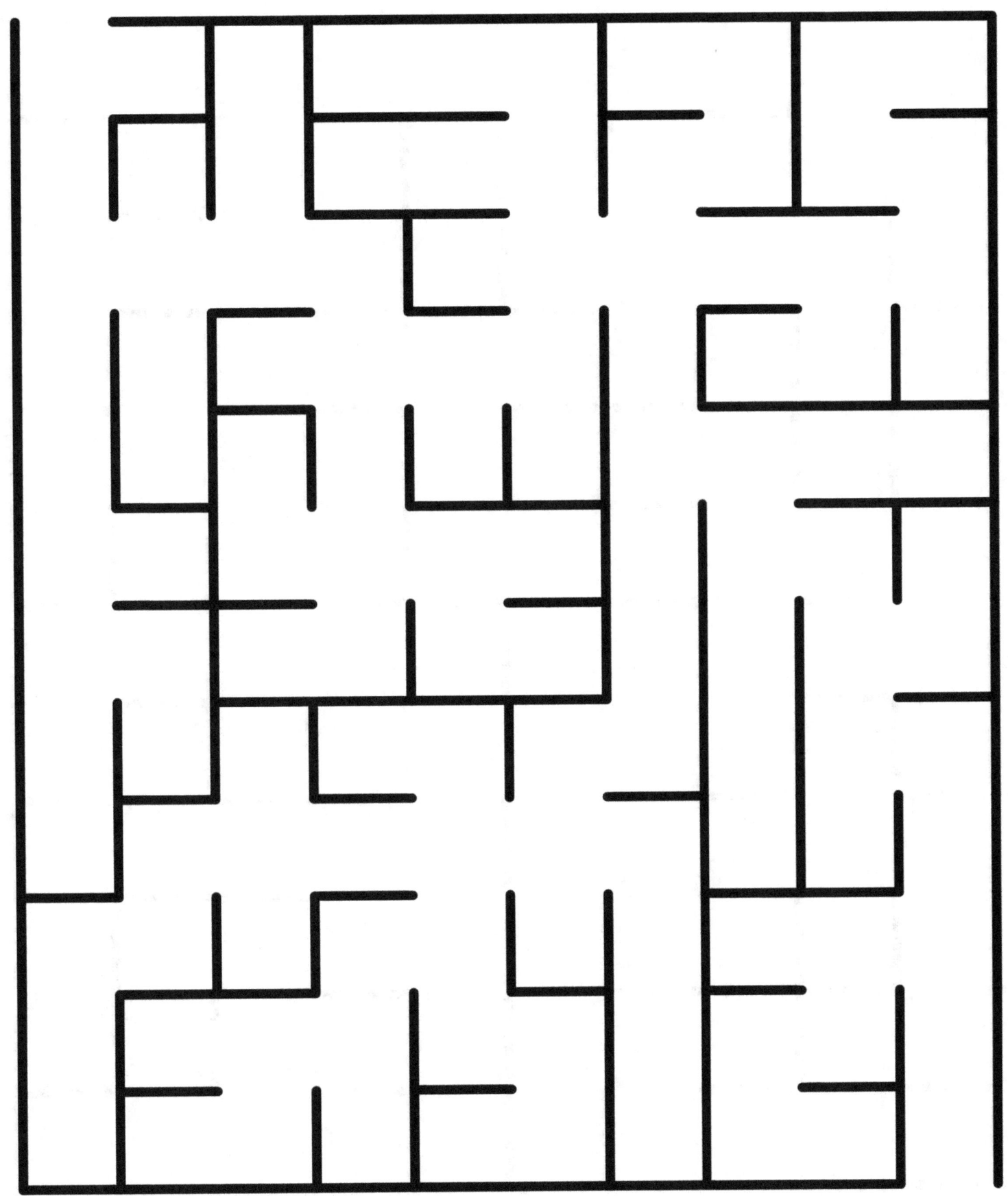

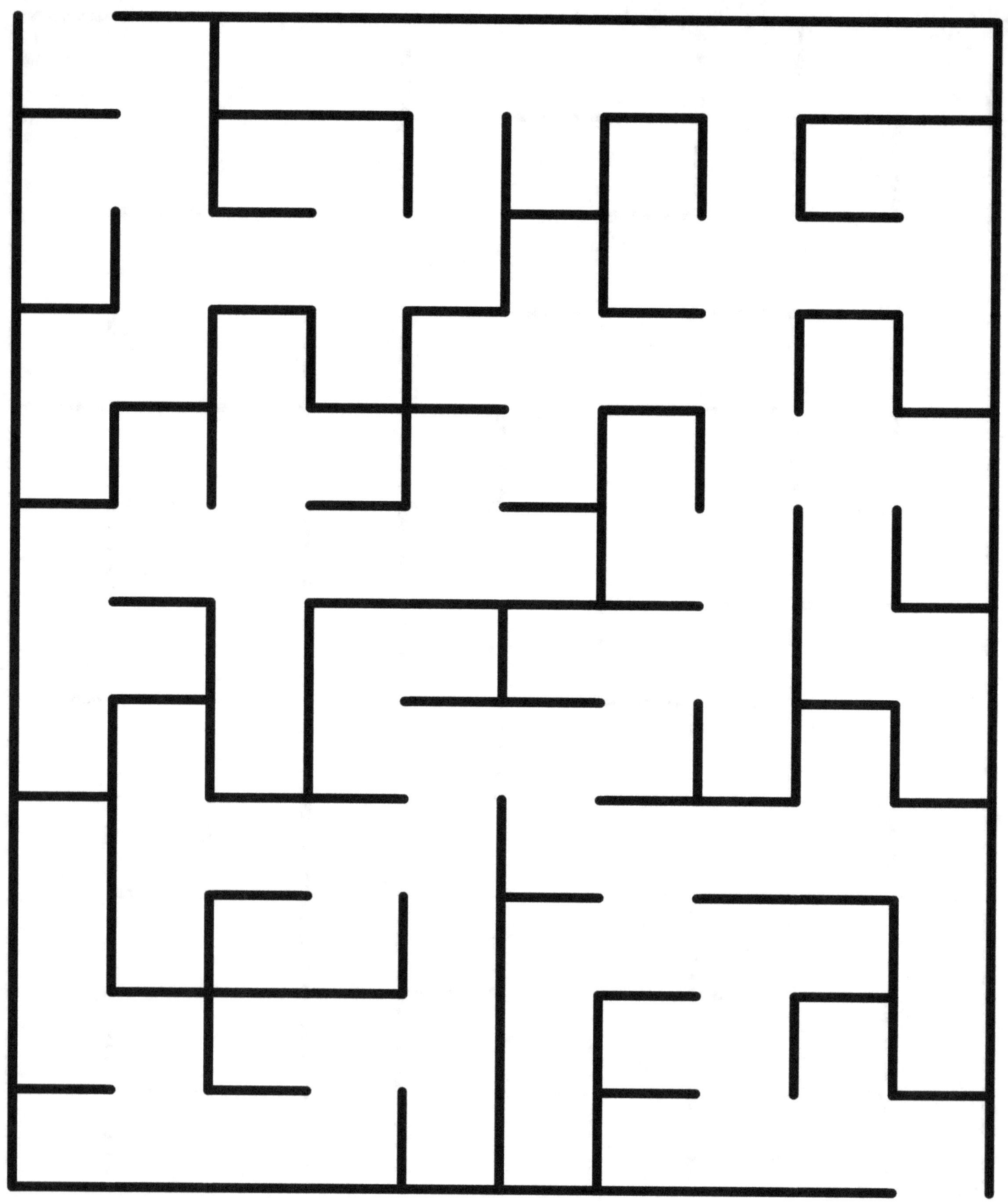

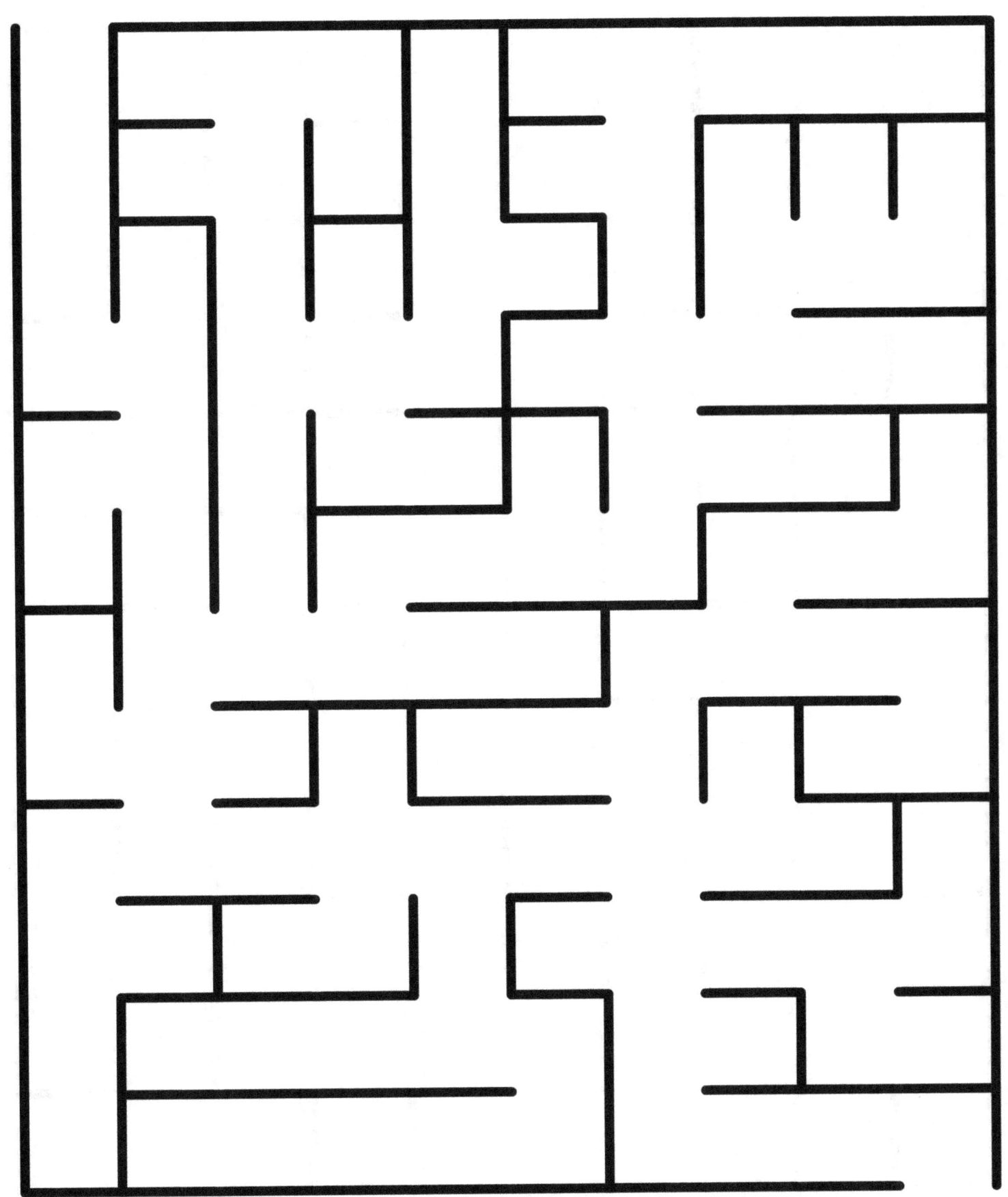

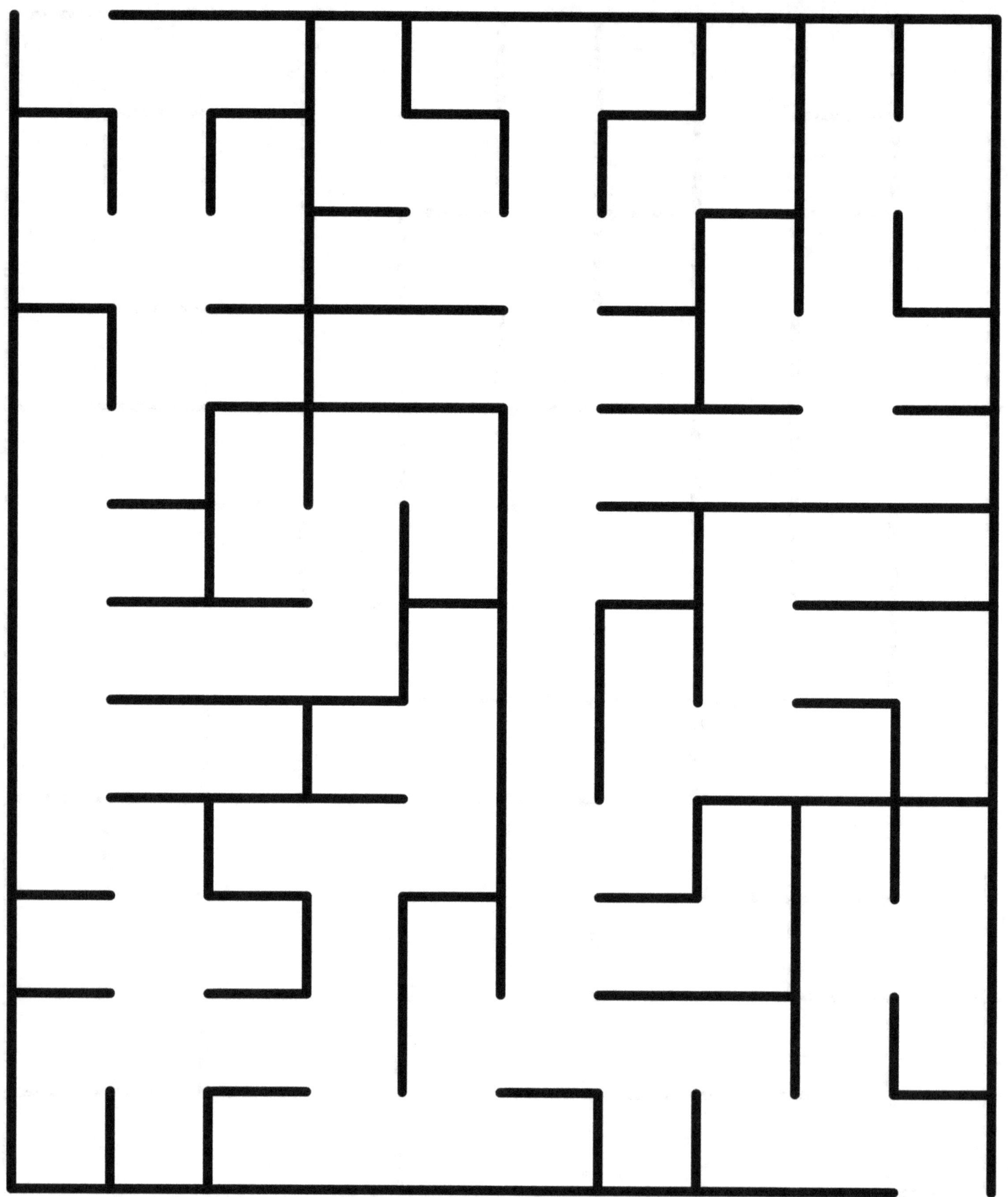

12×15 Easy Square Mazes

12×15 Medium Square Mazes

20×24 Medium Square Mazes

20×24 Hard Square Mazes

30×37 Hard Square Mazes

9×12 Easy Triangular Mazes

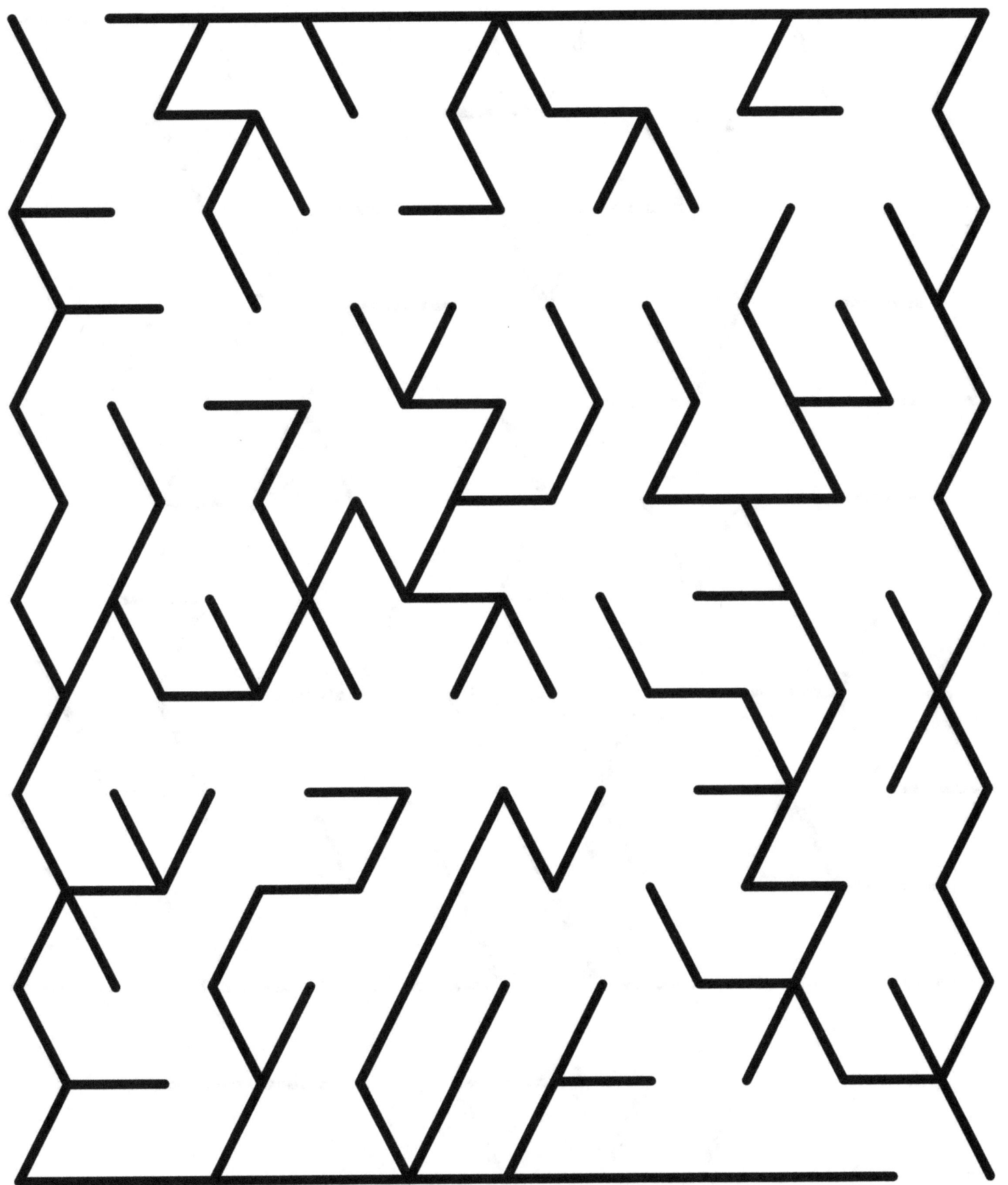

12×15 Easy Triangular Mazes

12×15 Medium Triangular Mazes

20×24 Medium Triangular Mazes

20×24 Hard Triangular Mazes

30×37 Hard Triangular Mazes

12×19 Easy Hexagonal Mazes

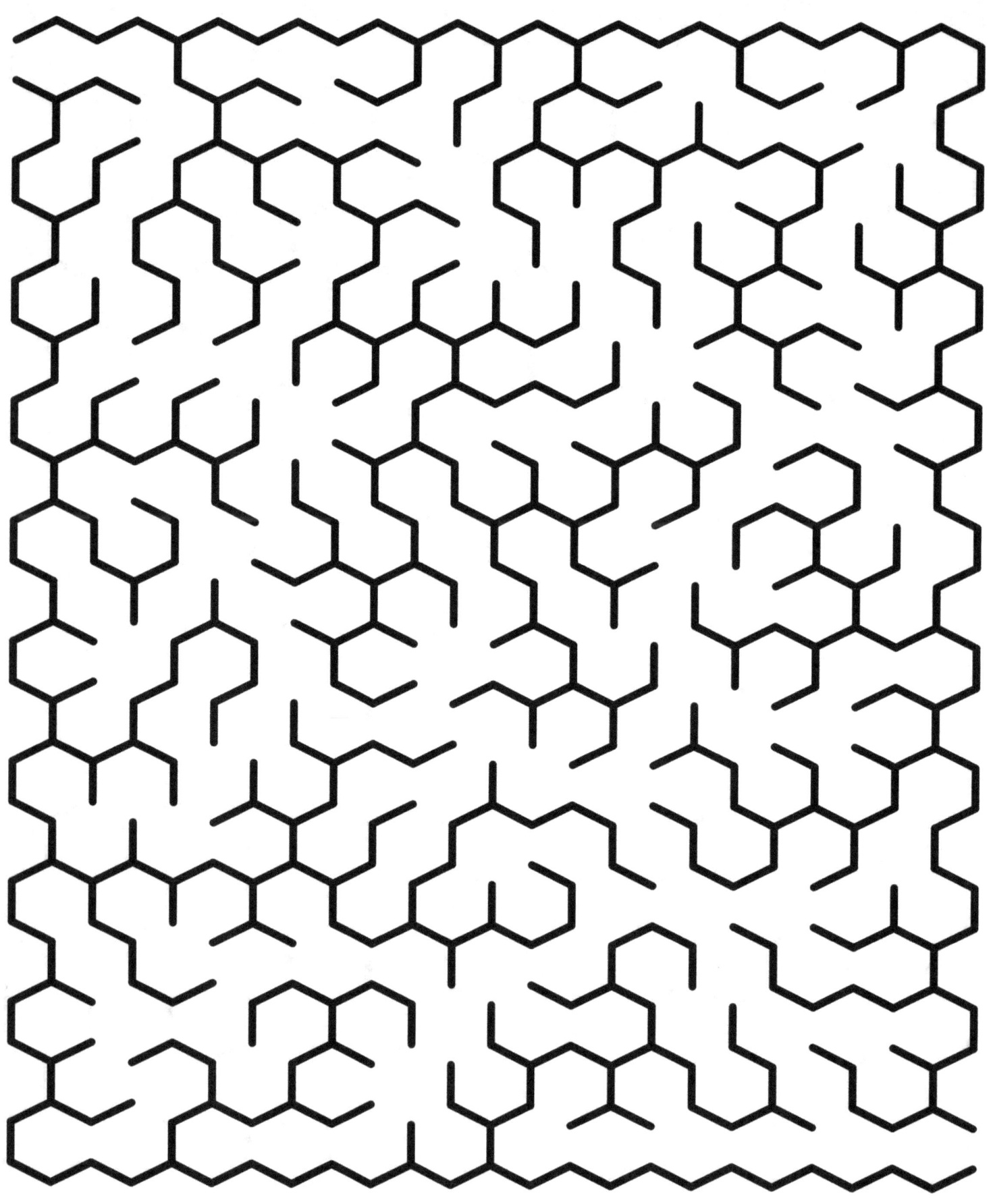

15×23 Easy Hexagonal Mazes

15×23 Medium Hexagonal Mazes

24×39 Medium Hexagonal Mazes

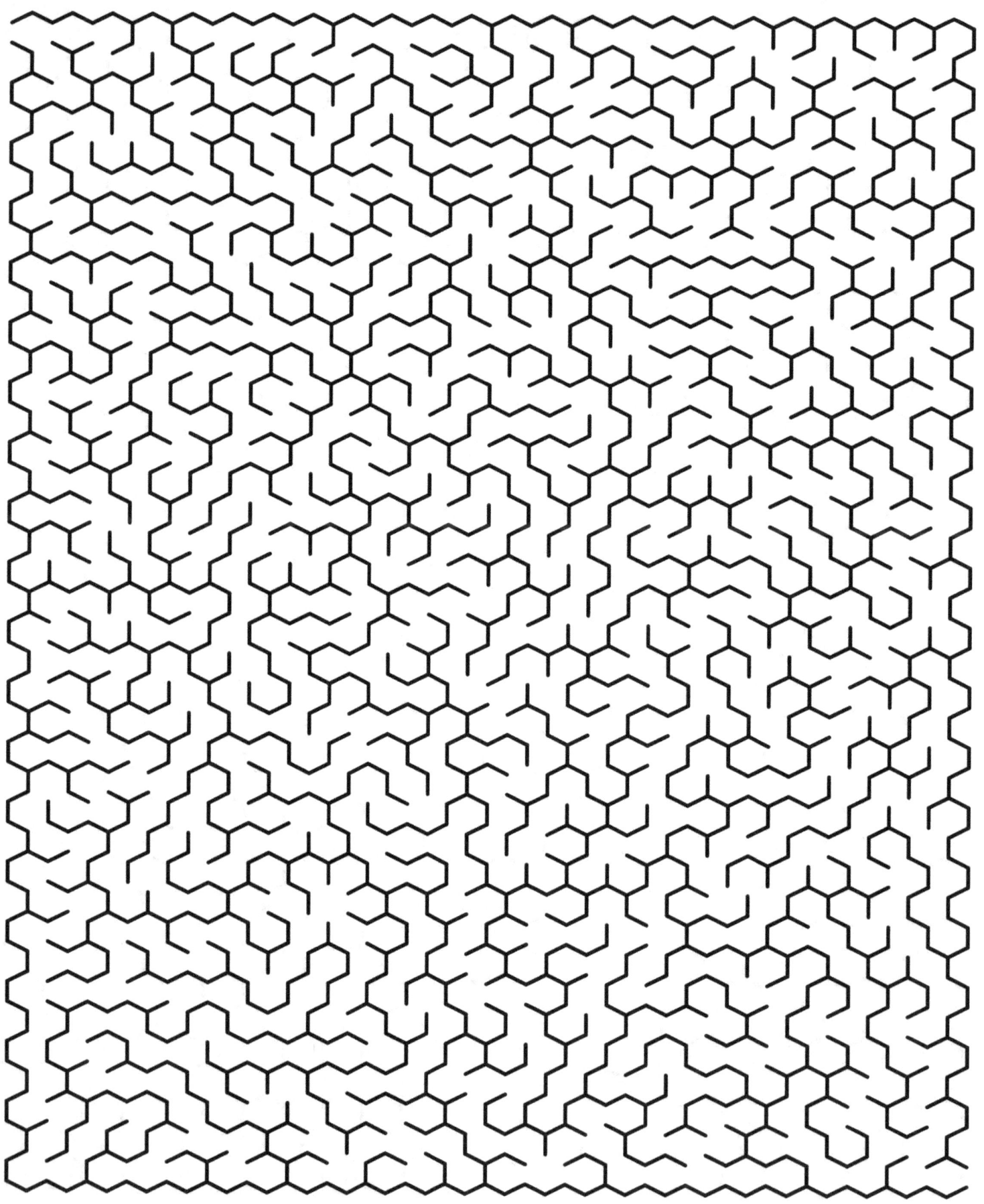

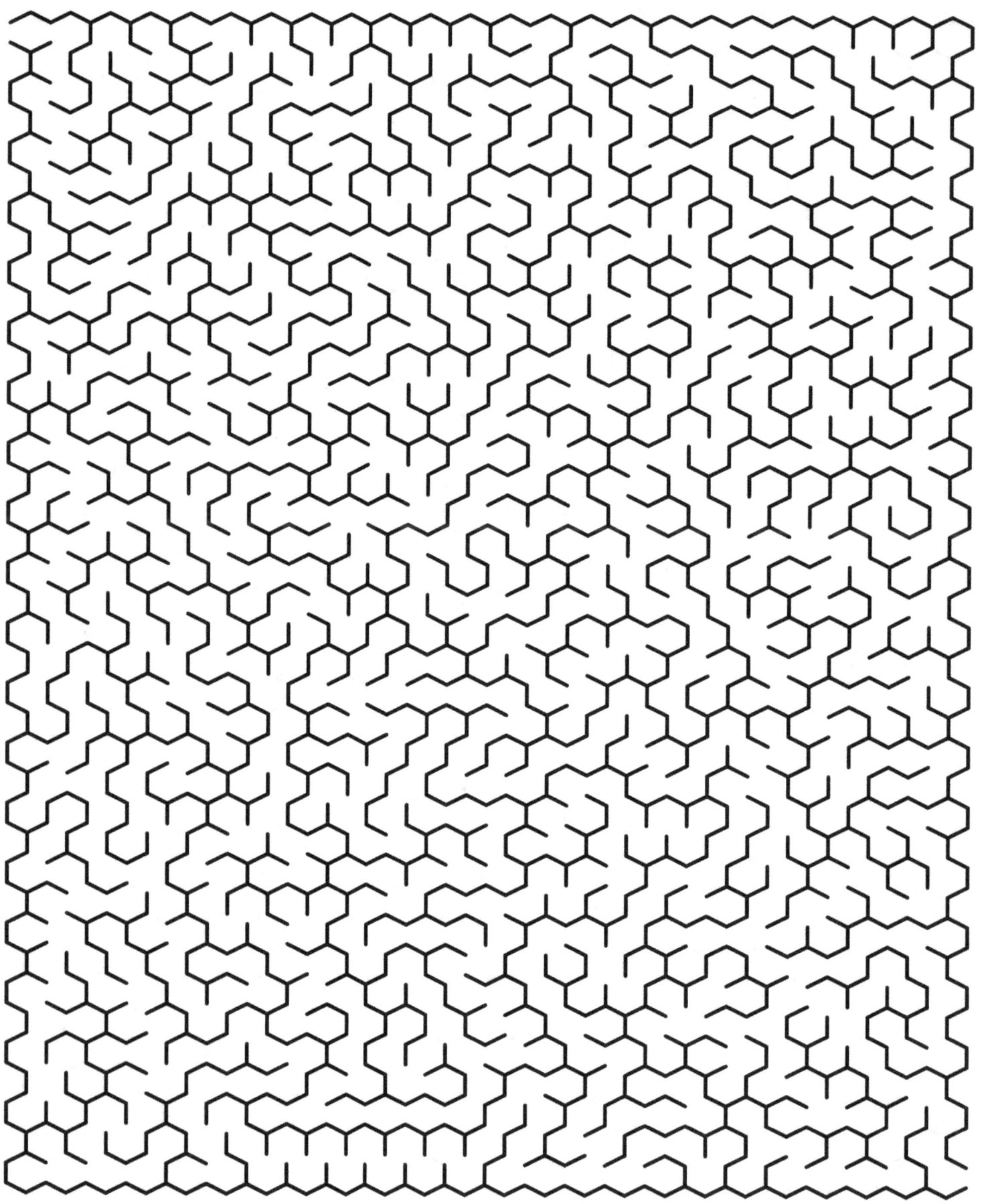

24×39 Hard Hexagonal Mazes

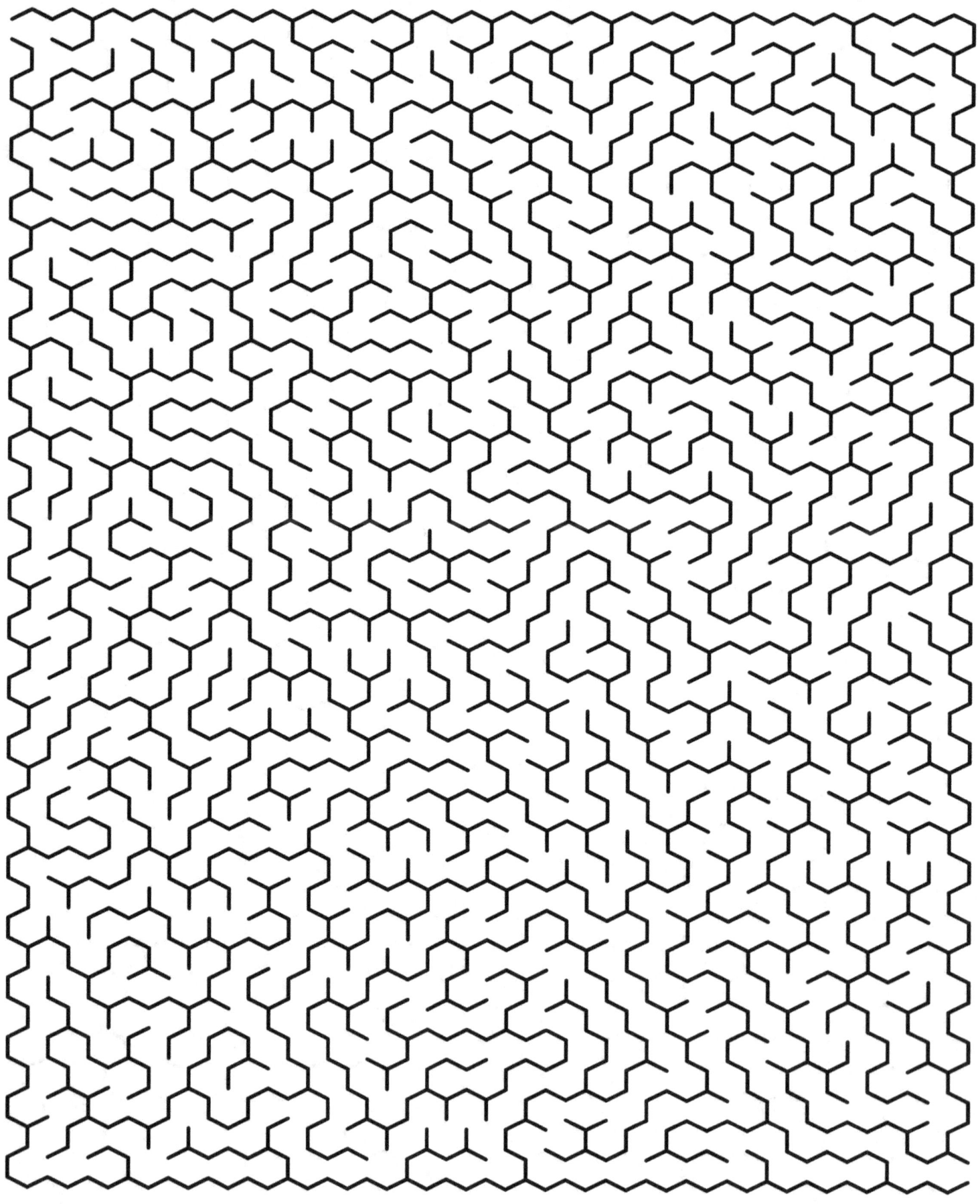

37×59 Hard Hexagonal Mazes

9×12 Easy Diamond Mazes

12×15 Easy Diamond Mazes

12×15 Medium Diamond Mazes

20×24 Medium Diamond Mazes

20×24 Hard Diamond Mazes

30×37 Hard Diamond Mazes

9×12 Easy Snub Square Mazes

12×15 Easy Snub Square Mazes

12×15 Medium Snub Square Mazes

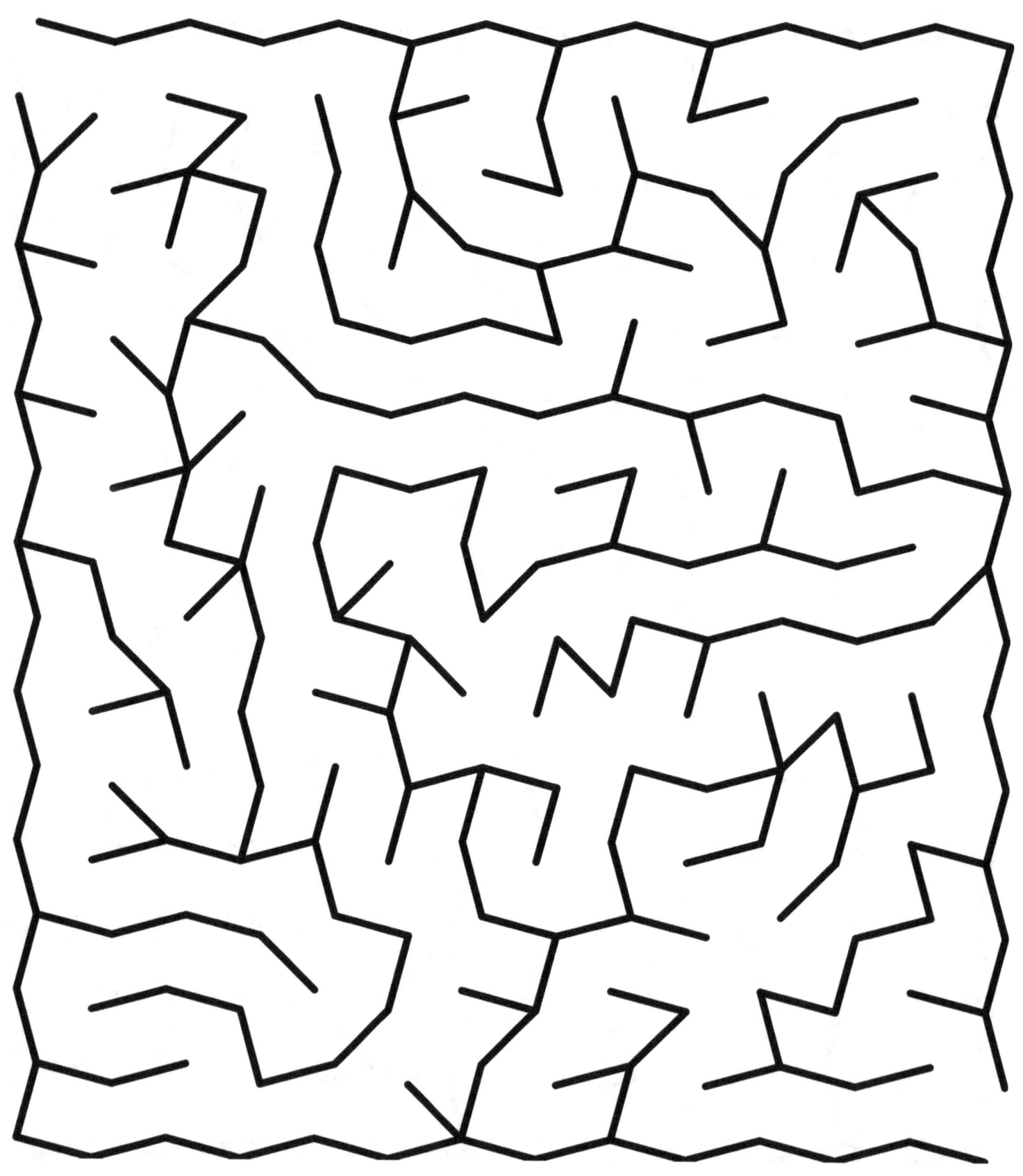

20×24 Medium Snub Square Mazes

20×24 Hard Snub Square Mazes

30×37 Hard Snub Square Mazes

9×12 Easy Snub Square 2 Mazes

9×12 Easy Cairo Mazes

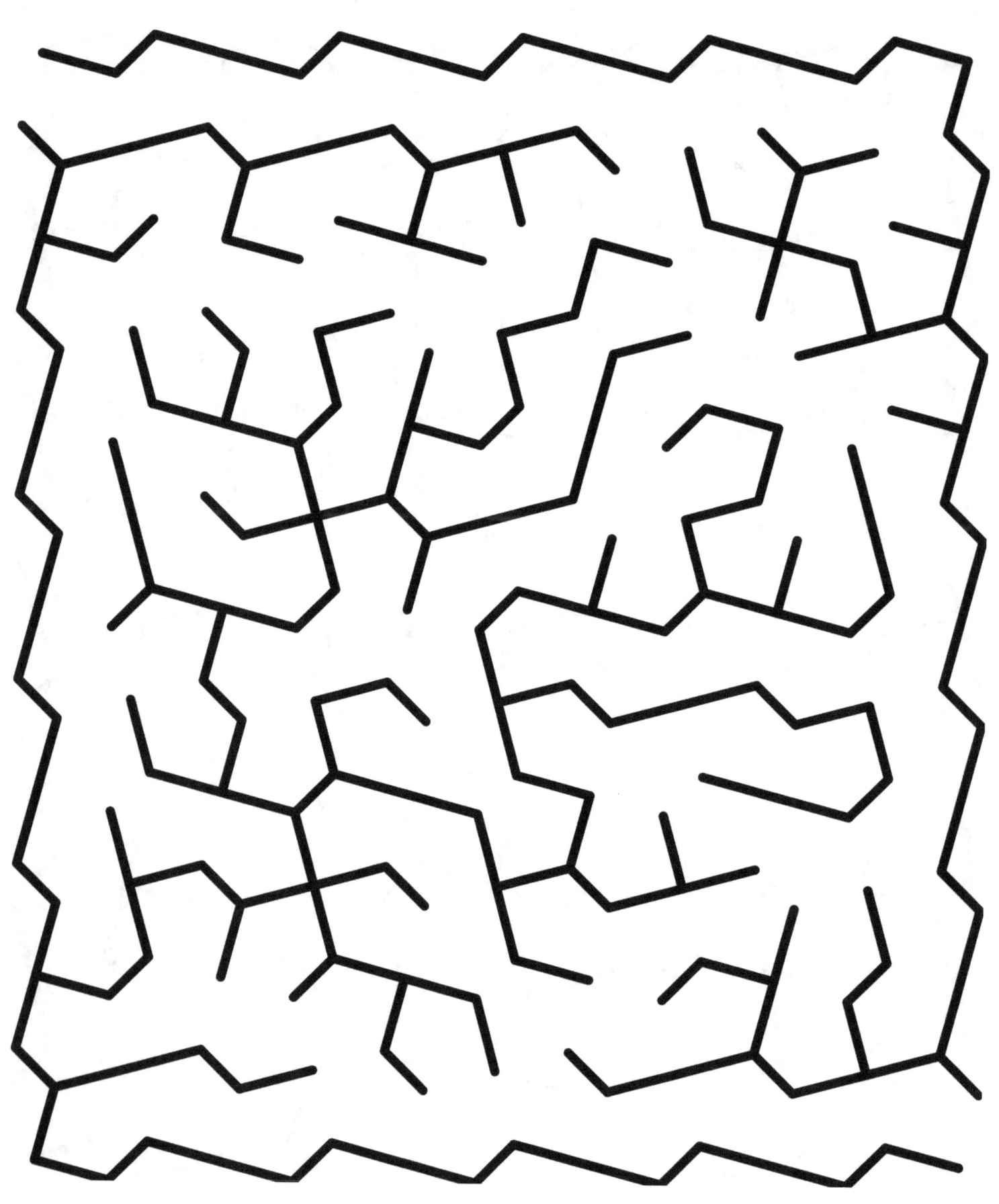

12×15 Easy Cairo Mazes

13×16 Easy Cairo Mazes

13×15 Medium Cairo Mazes

20×24 Medium Cairo Mazes

20×24 Hard Cairo Mazes

30×37 Hard Cairo Mazes

20×20 Hard Circular Mazes

25×25 Hard Circular Mazes

30×30 Hard Circular Mazes

35×35 Hard Circular Mazes

9×12 Easy Square Triangle Mazes

12×15 Easy Square Triangle Mazes

12×15 Medium Square Triangle Mazes

20×24 Medium Square Triangle Mazes

20×24 Hard Square Triangle Mazes

30×37 Hard Square Triangle Mazes

Solutions

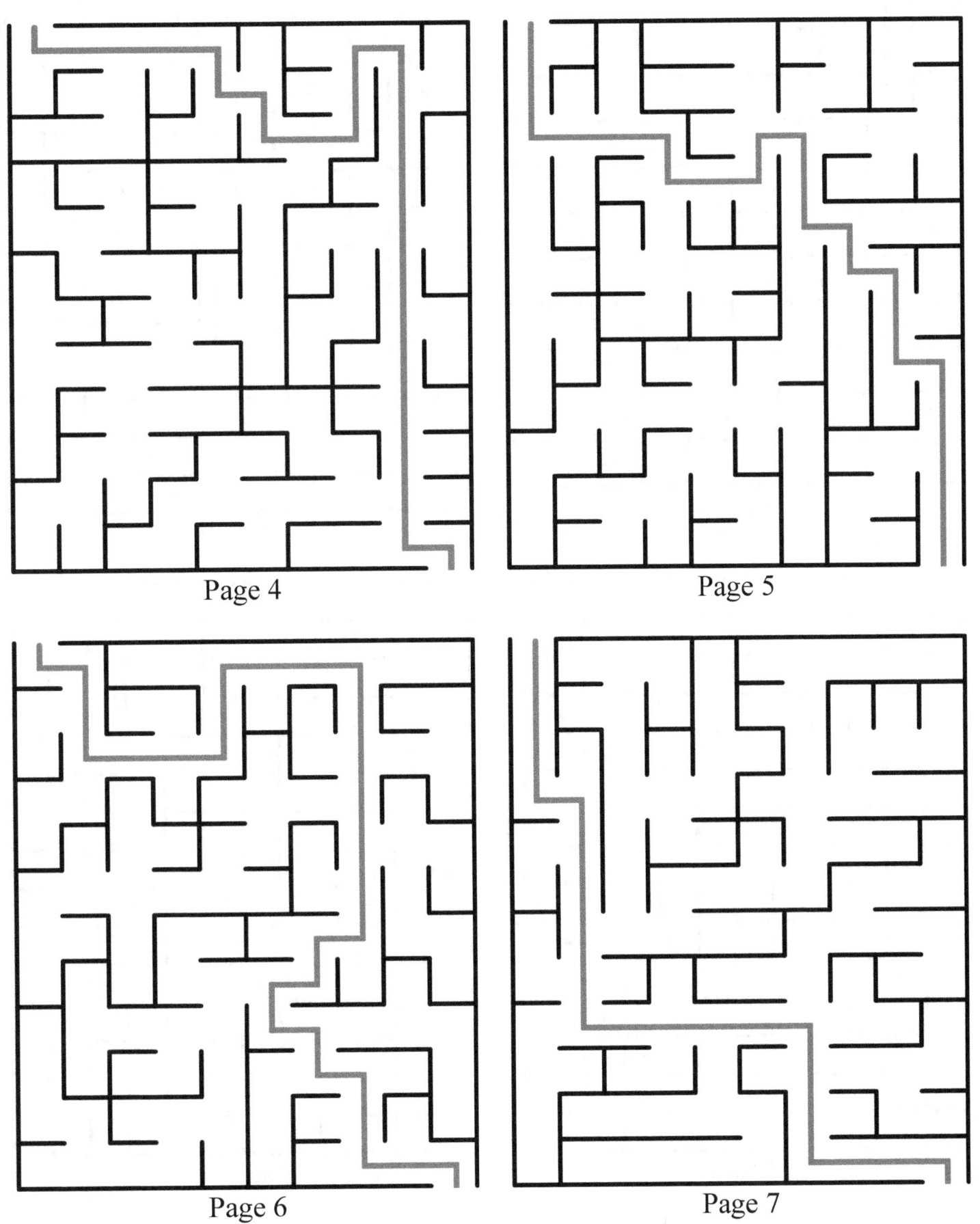

Page 4

Page 5

Page 6

Page 7

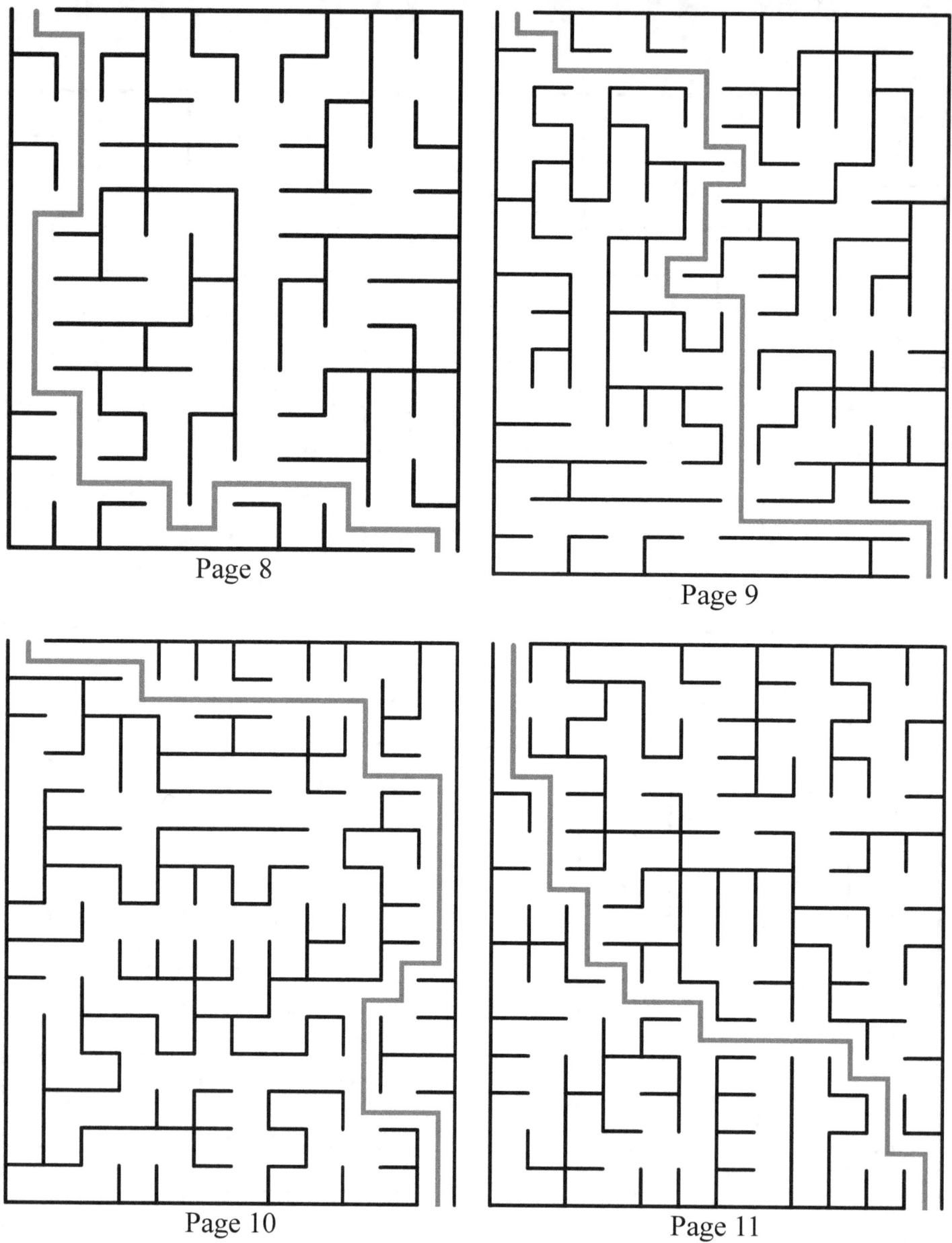

Page 12 Page 13

Page 14 Page 15

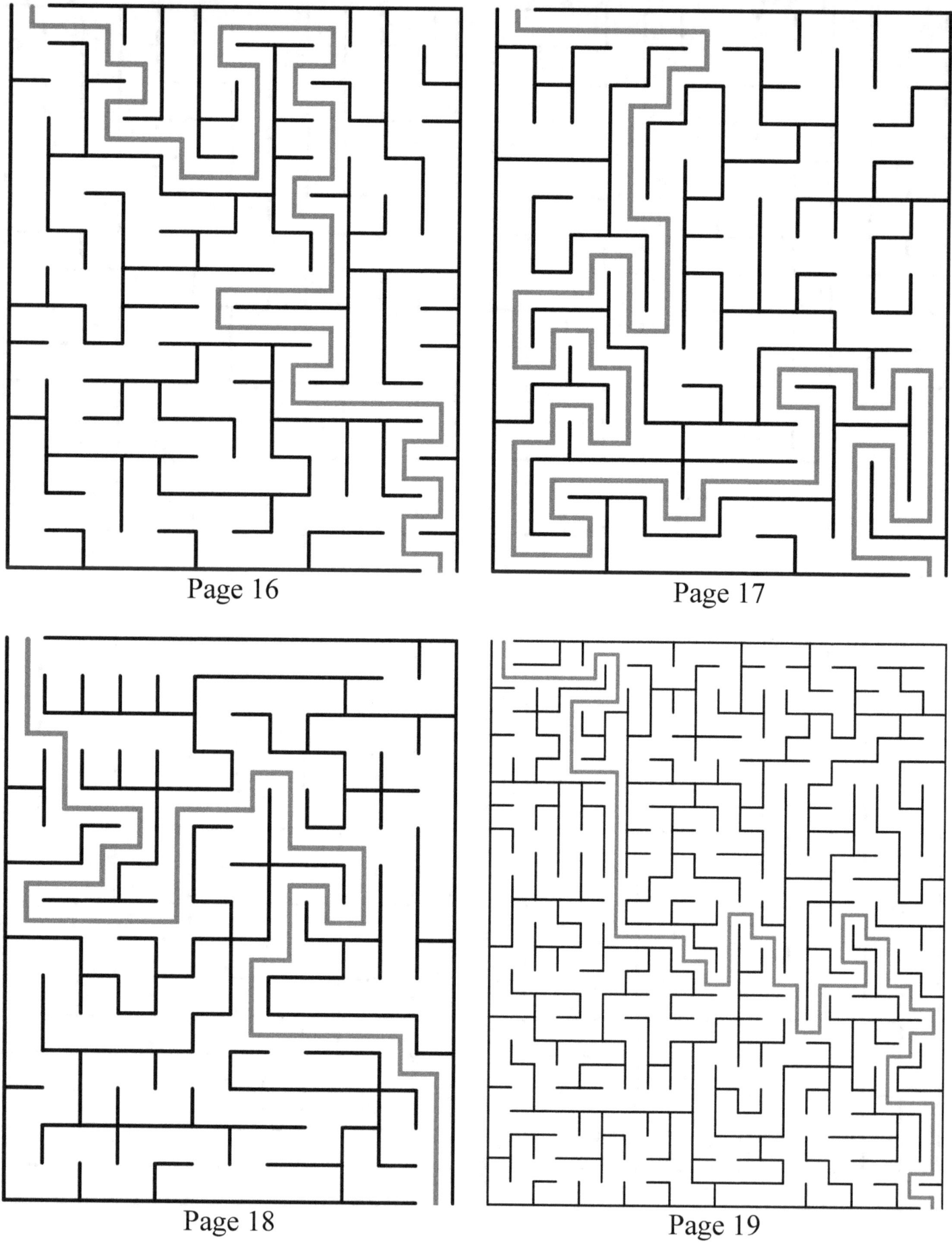

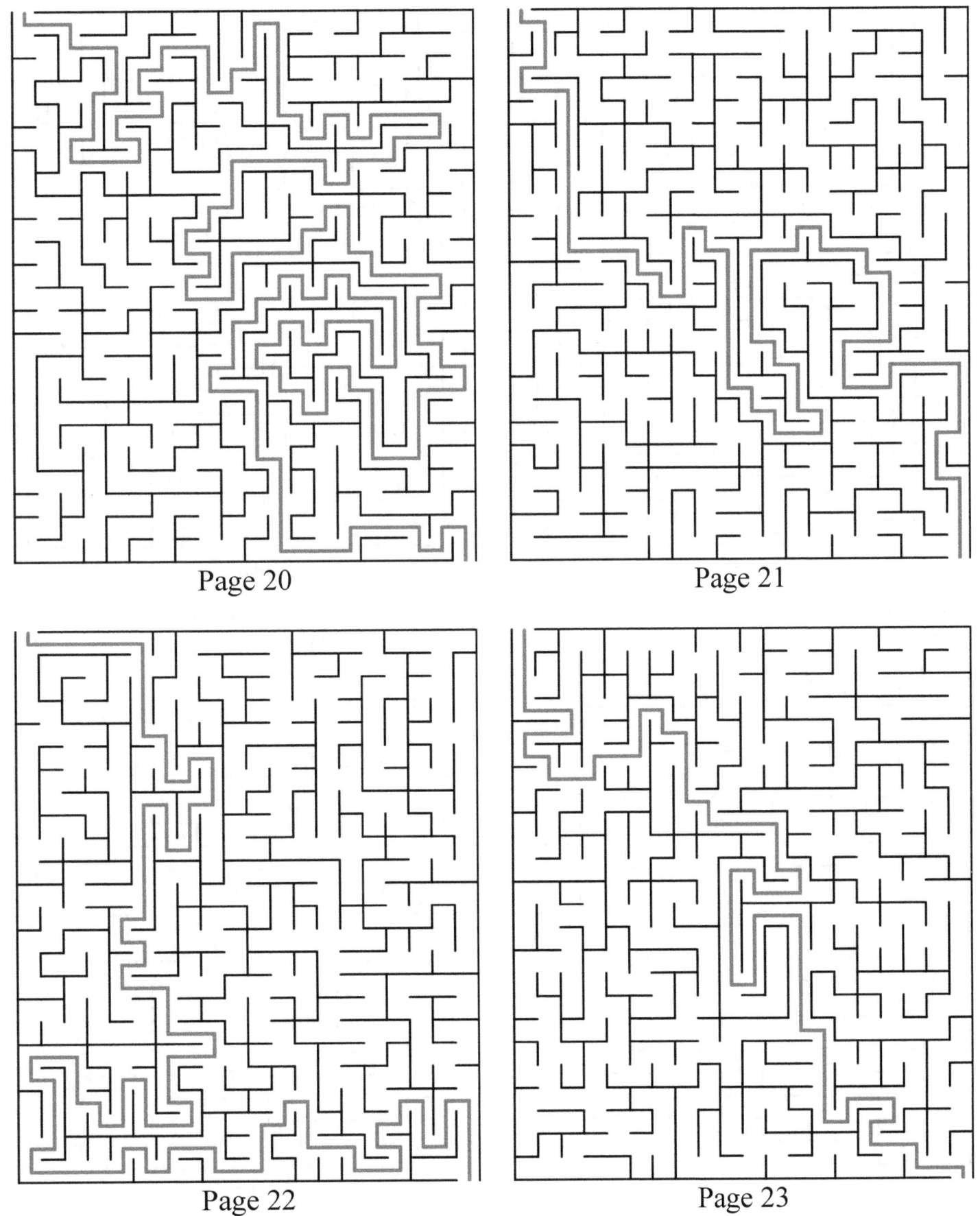

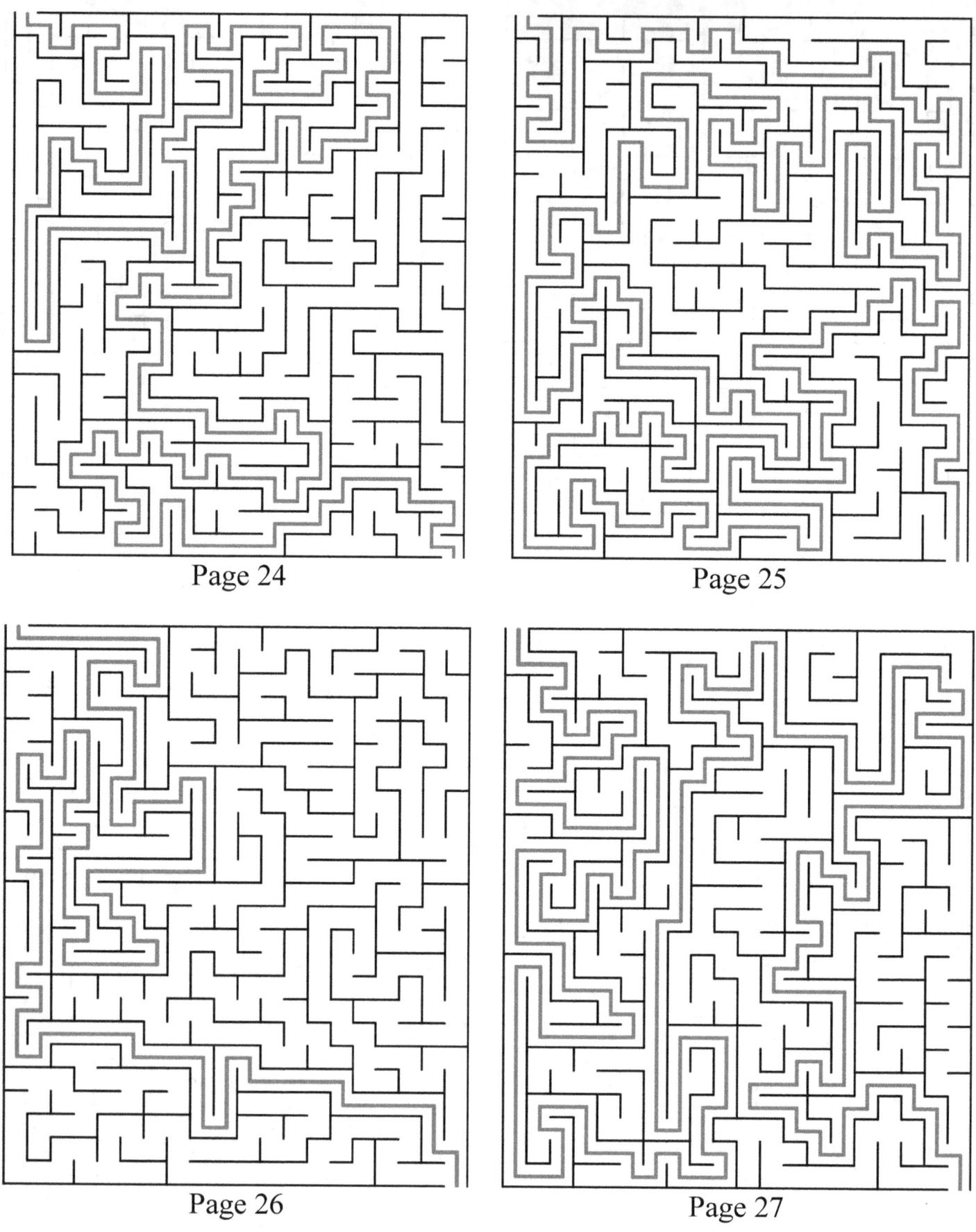

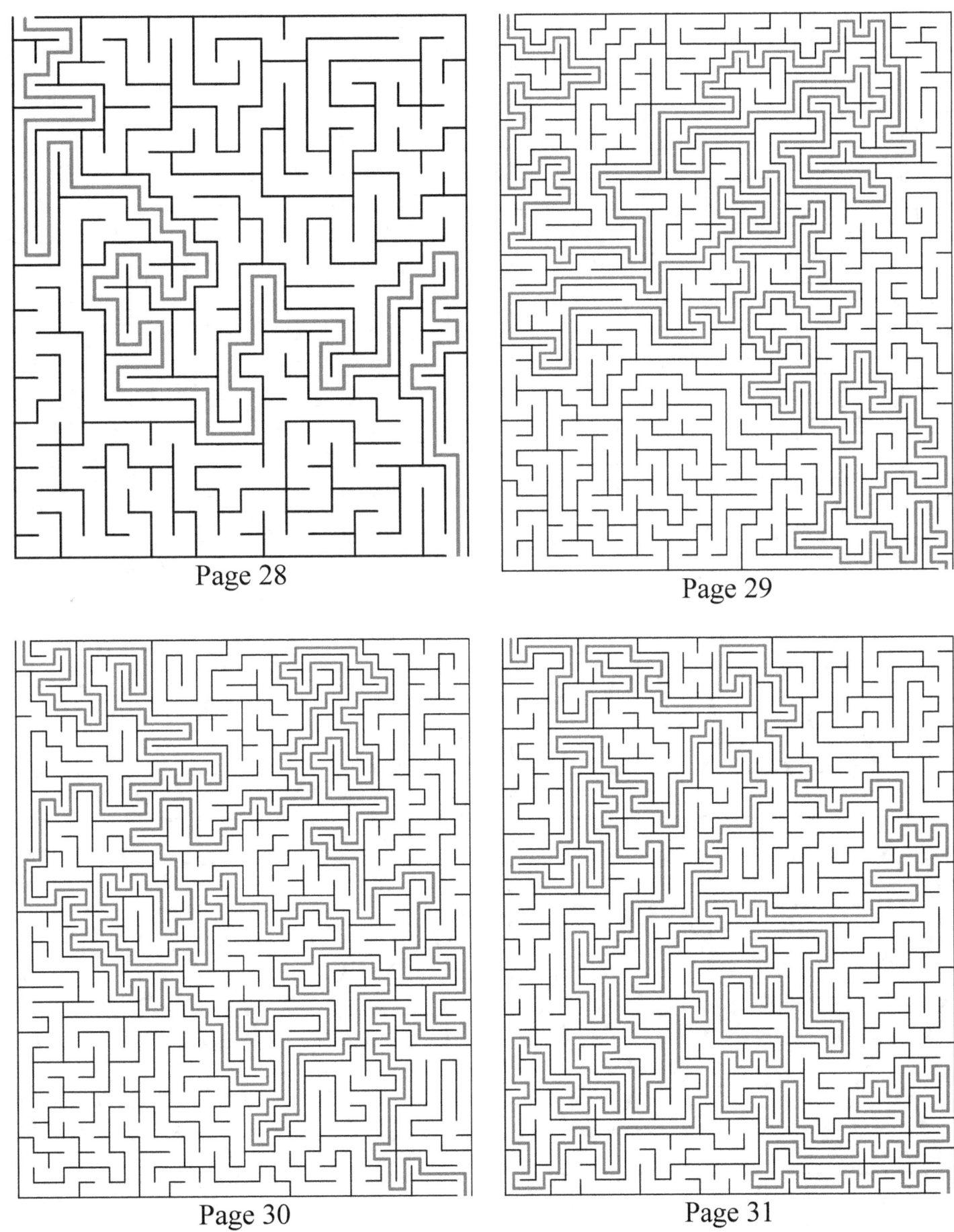

Page 28

Page 29

Page 30

Page 31

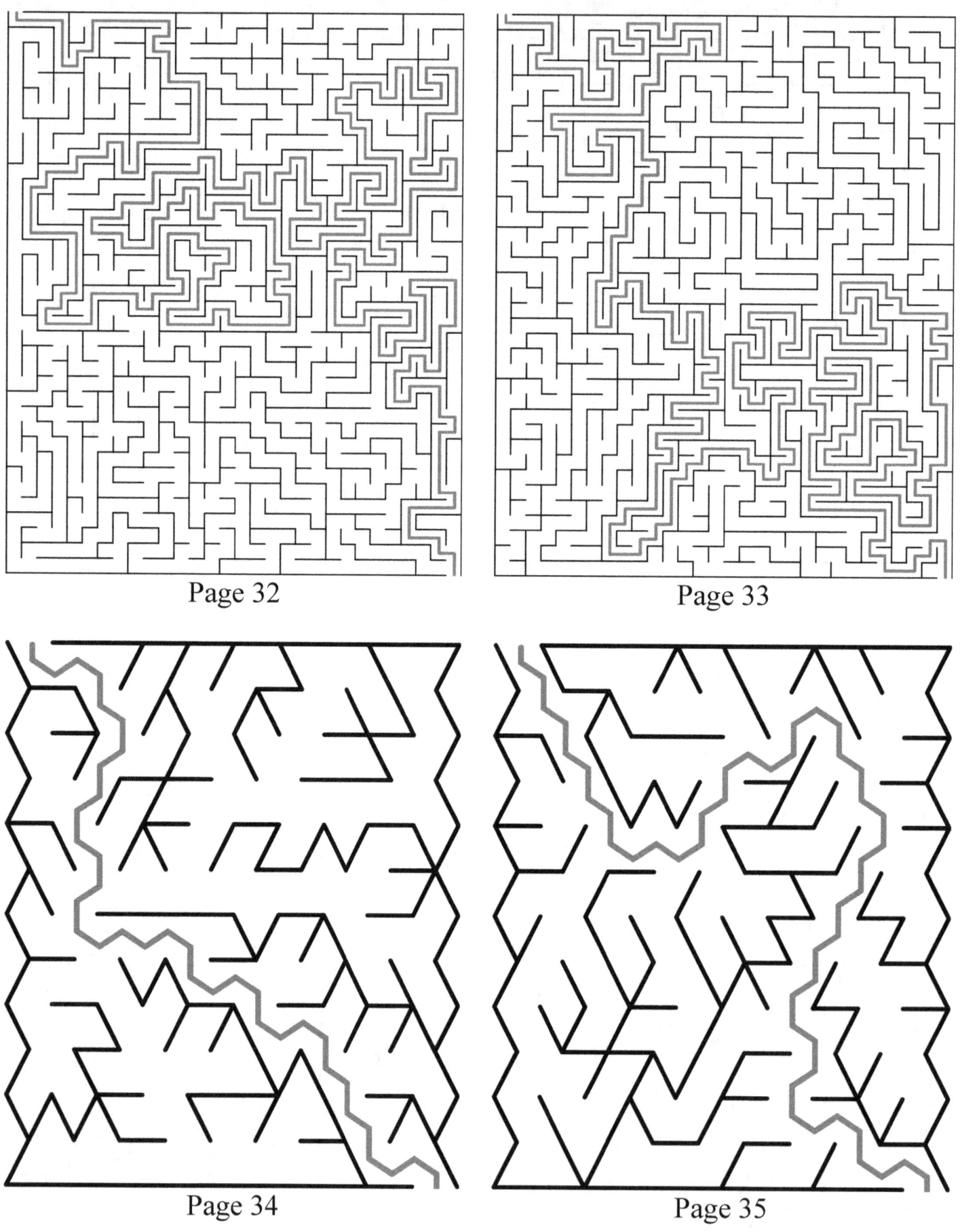

Page 44 Page 45

Page 46 Page 47

Page 52

Page 53

Page 54

Page 55

Mazes Galore! Copyright 2025 Life is a Story Problem. All rights reserved. 257

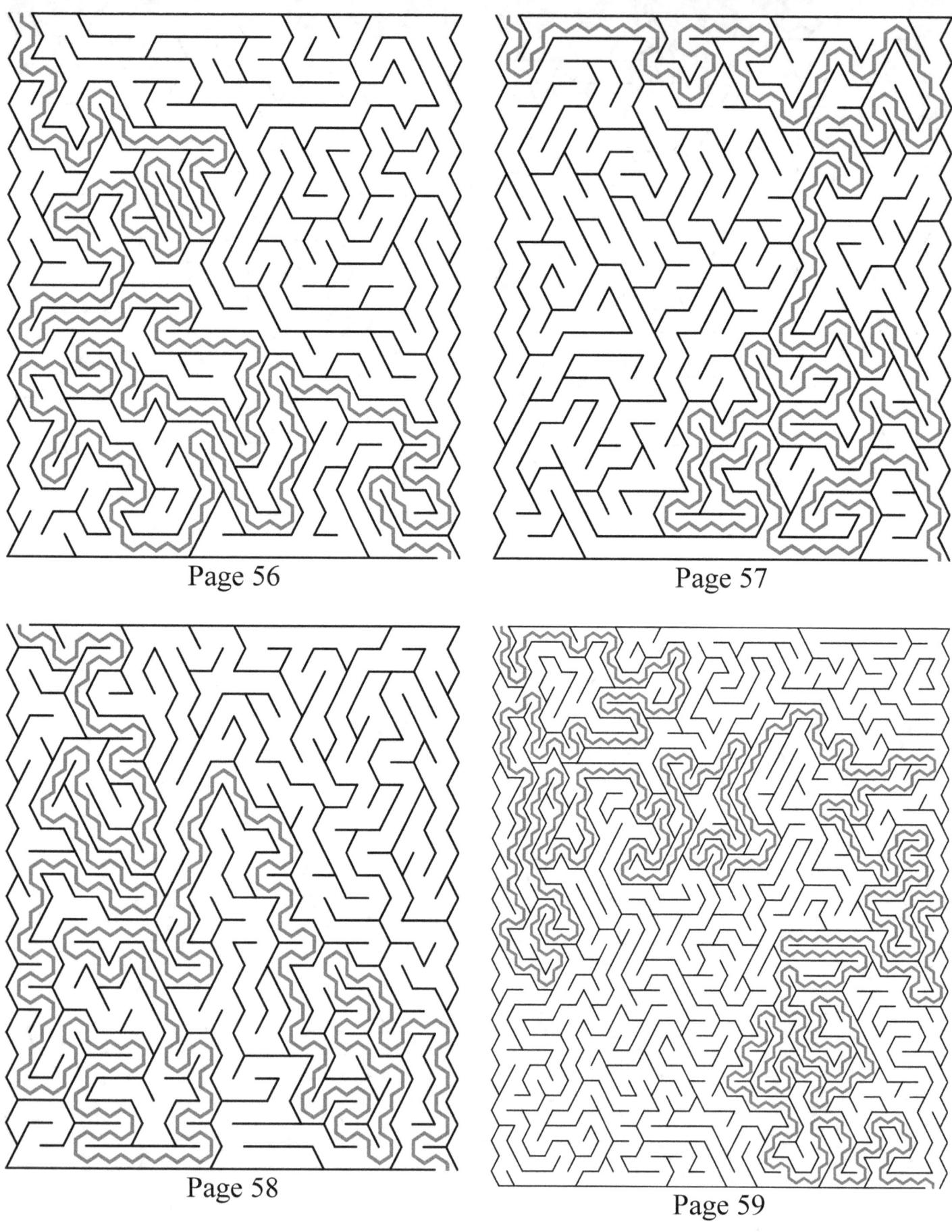

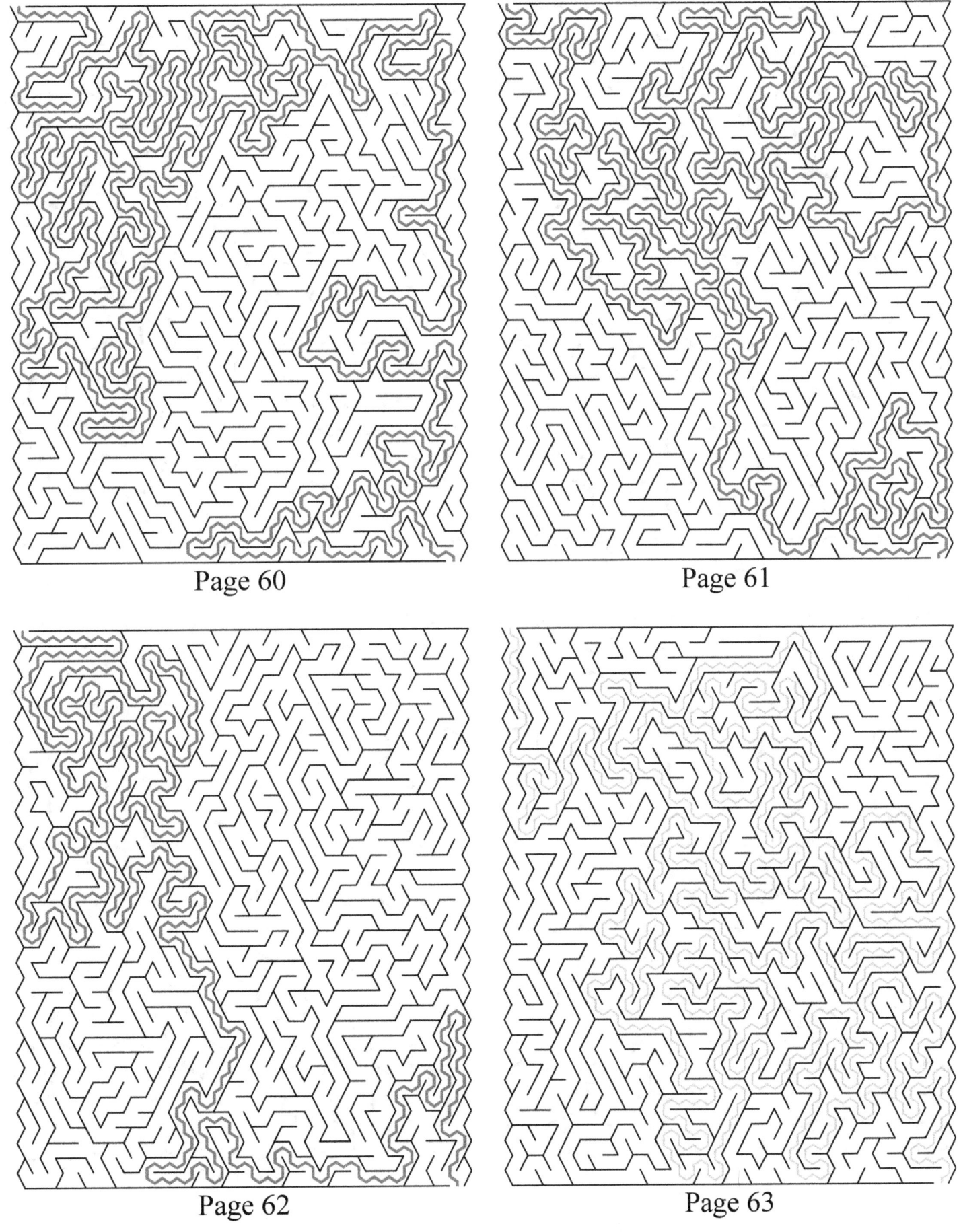

Page 60

Page 61

Page 62

Page 63

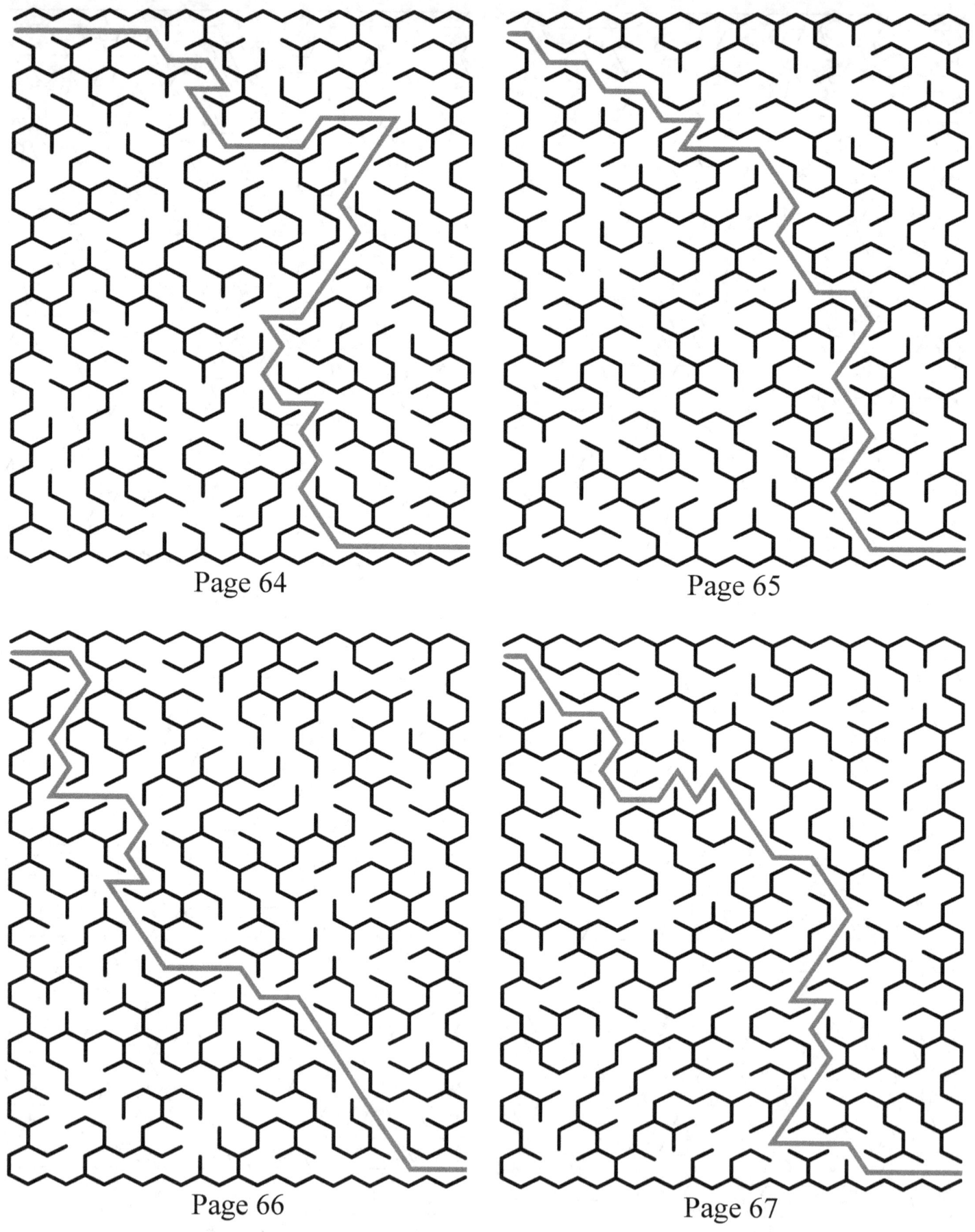

Page 64

Page 65

Page 66

Page 67

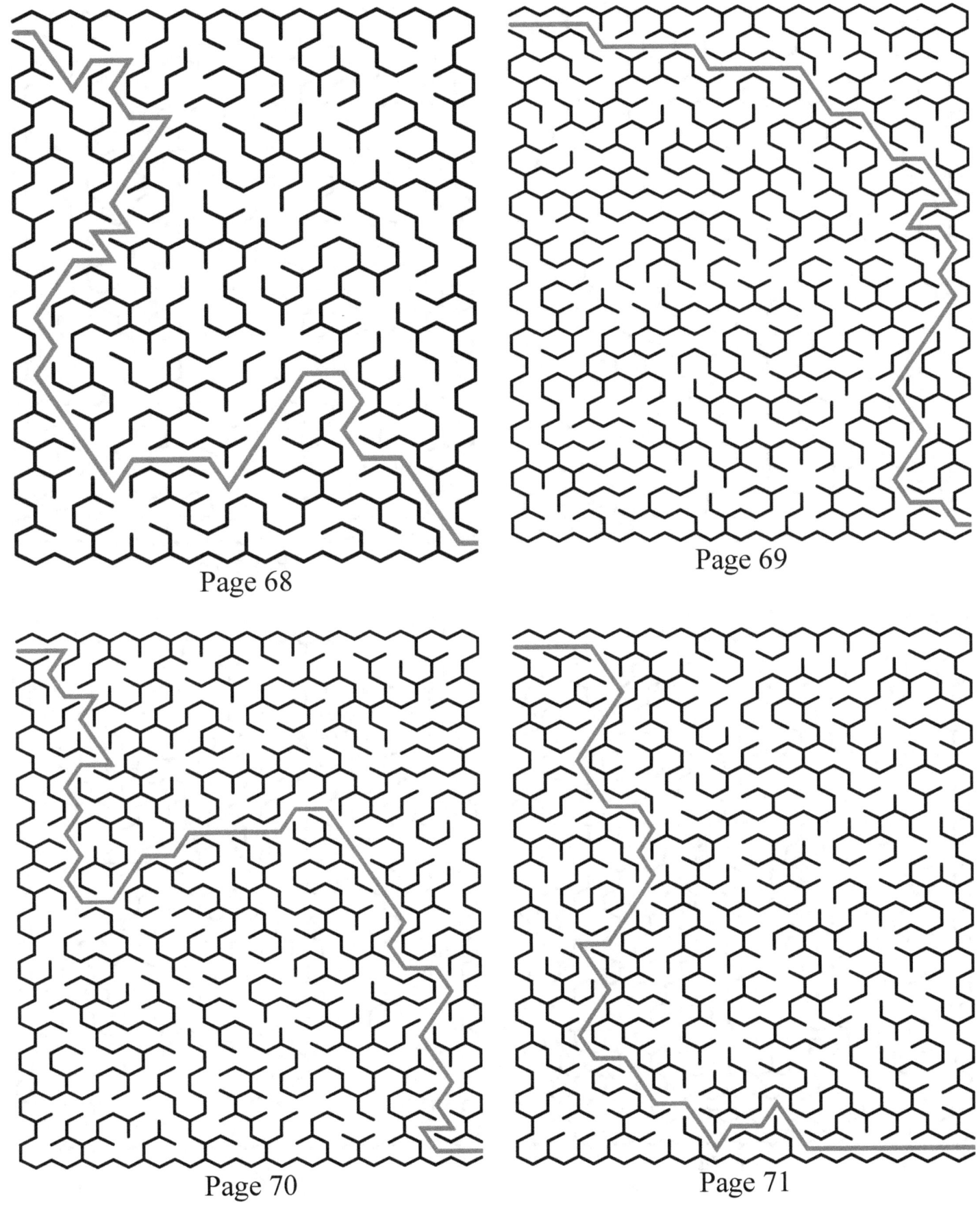

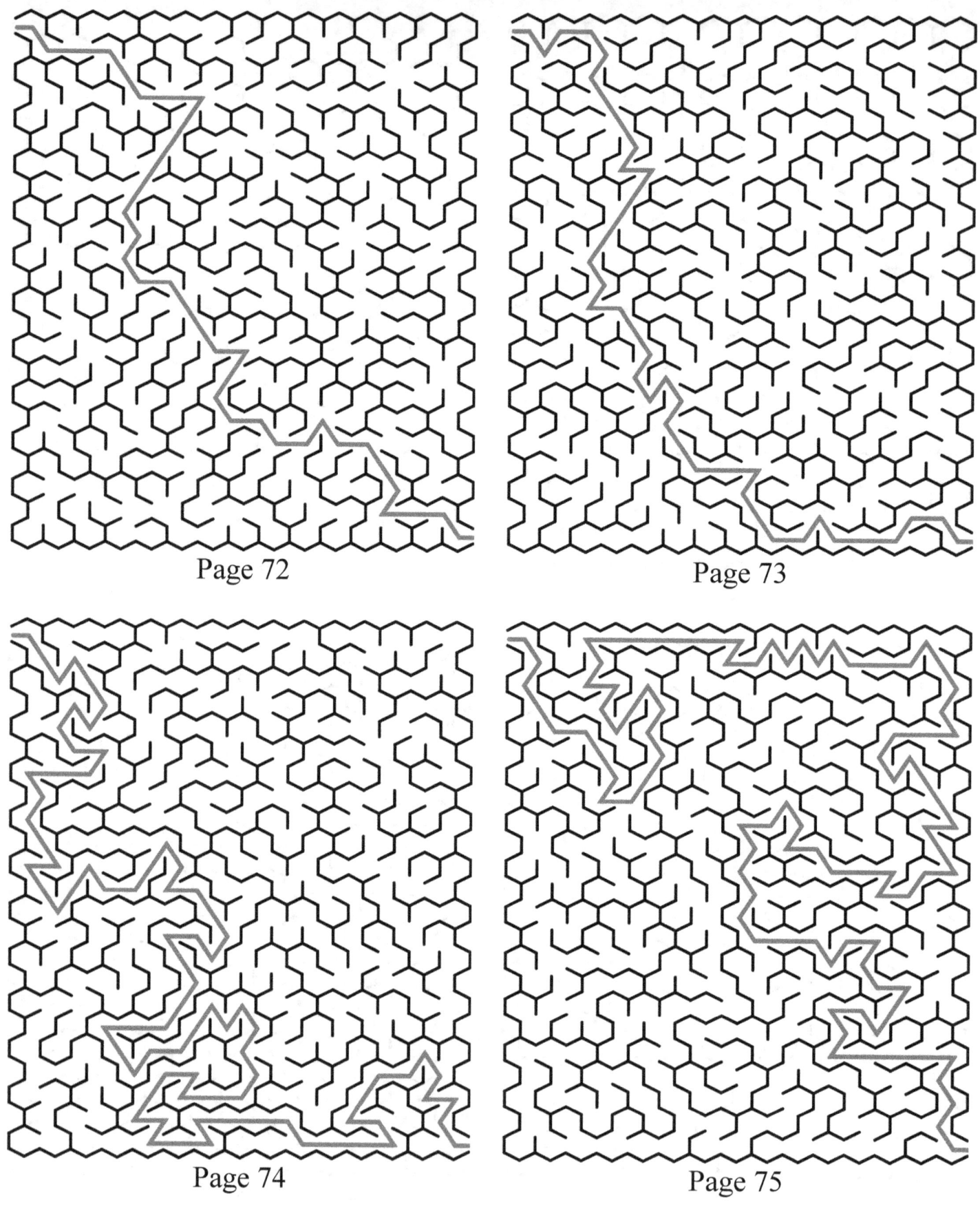

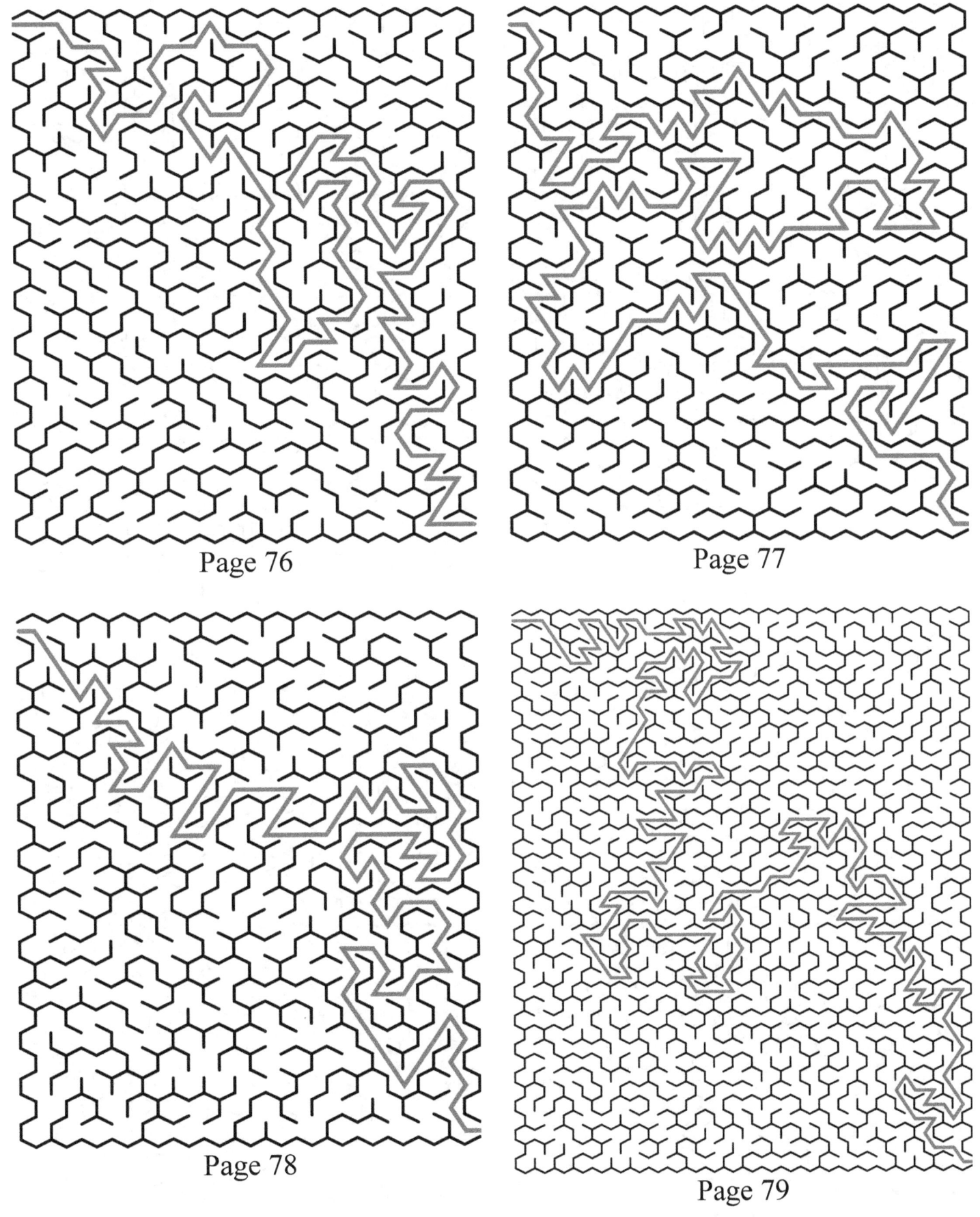

Page 76

Page 77

Page 78

Page 79

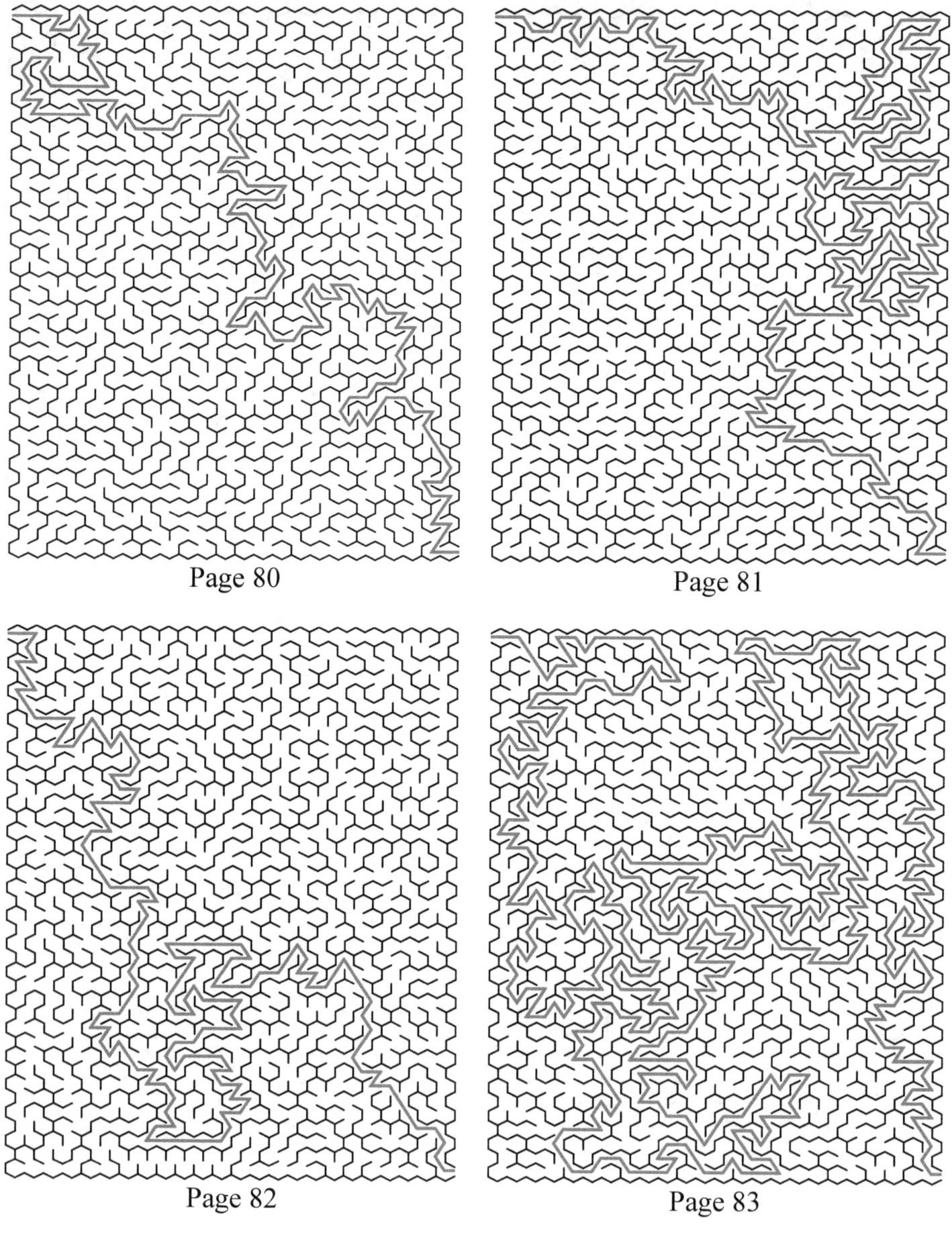

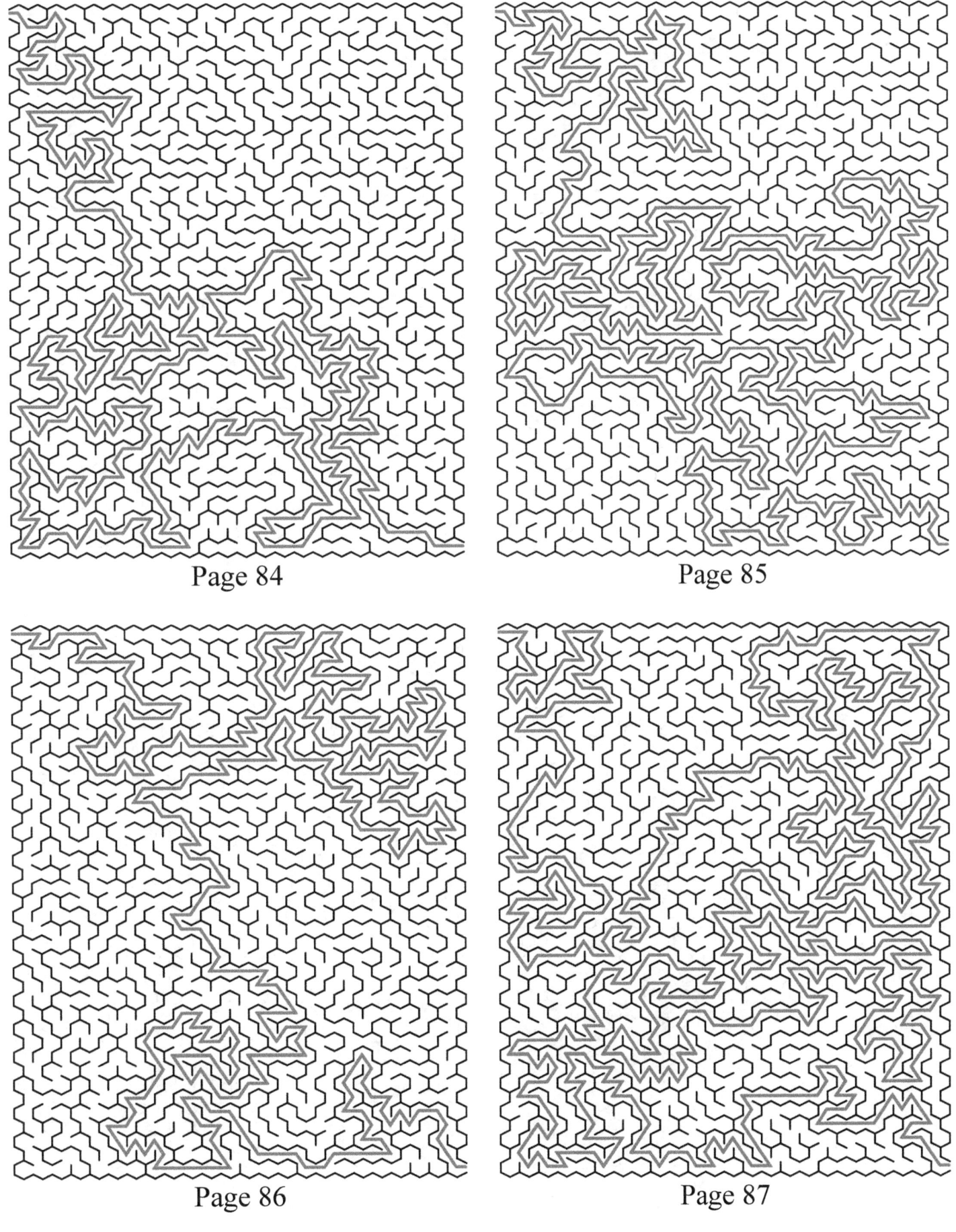

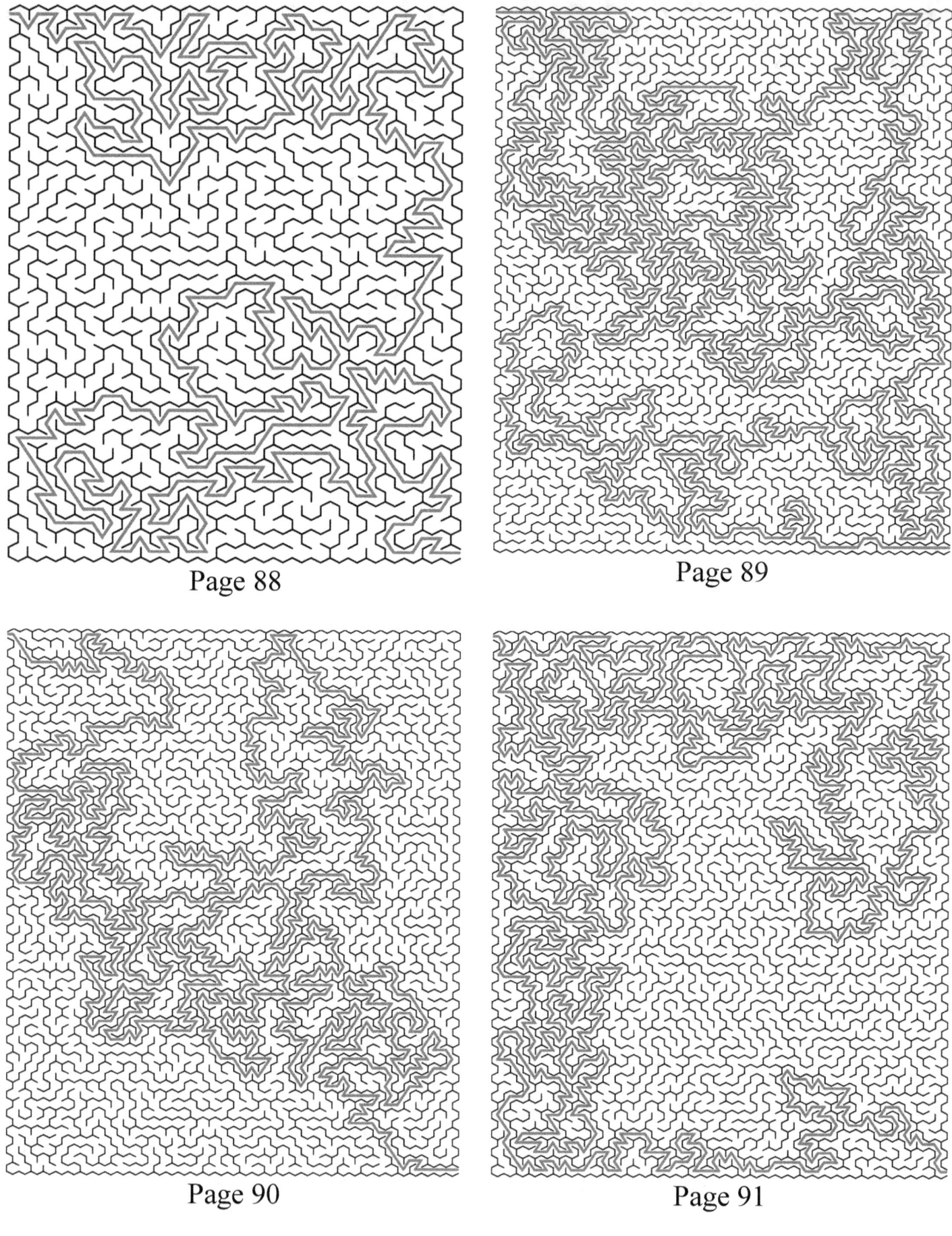

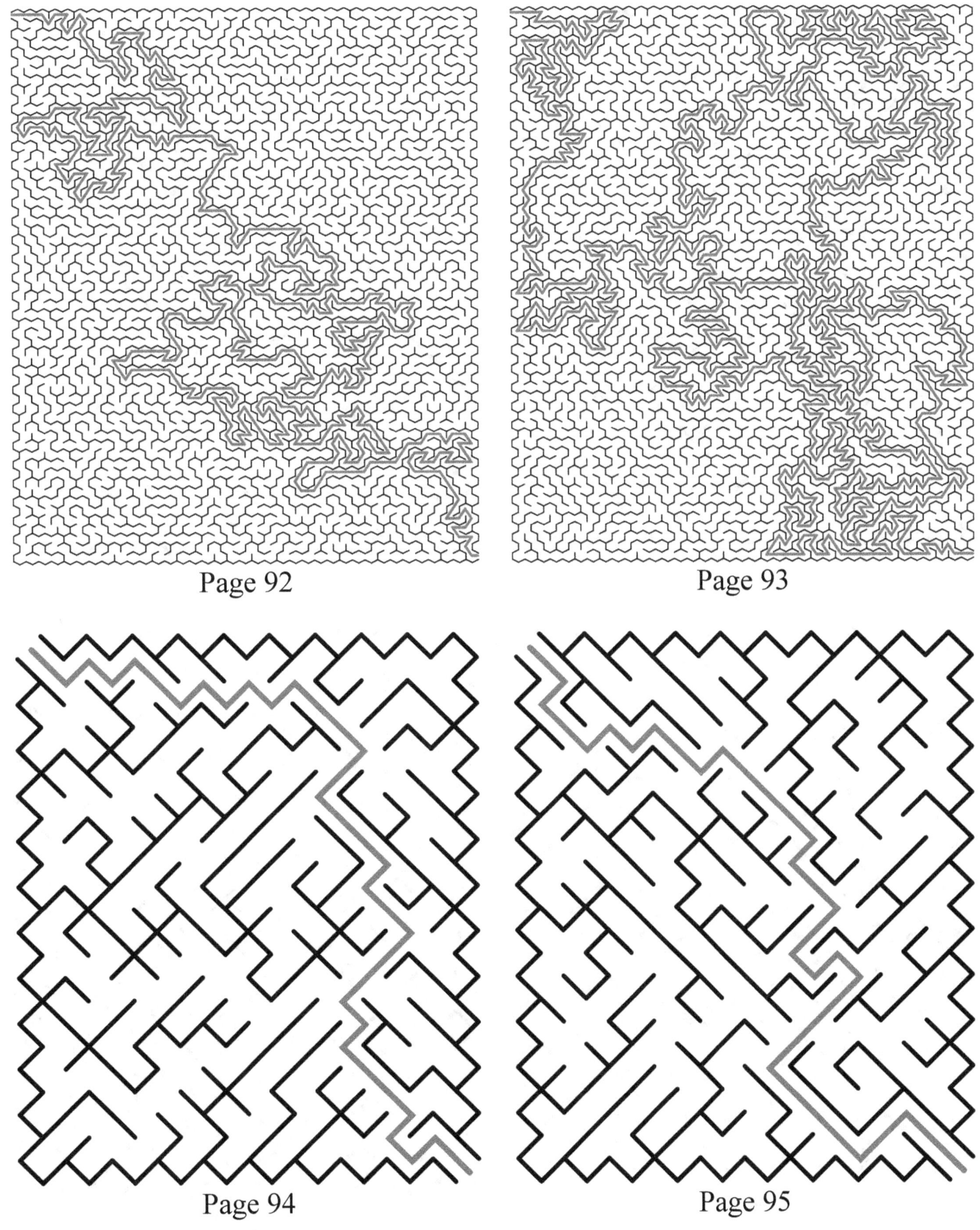

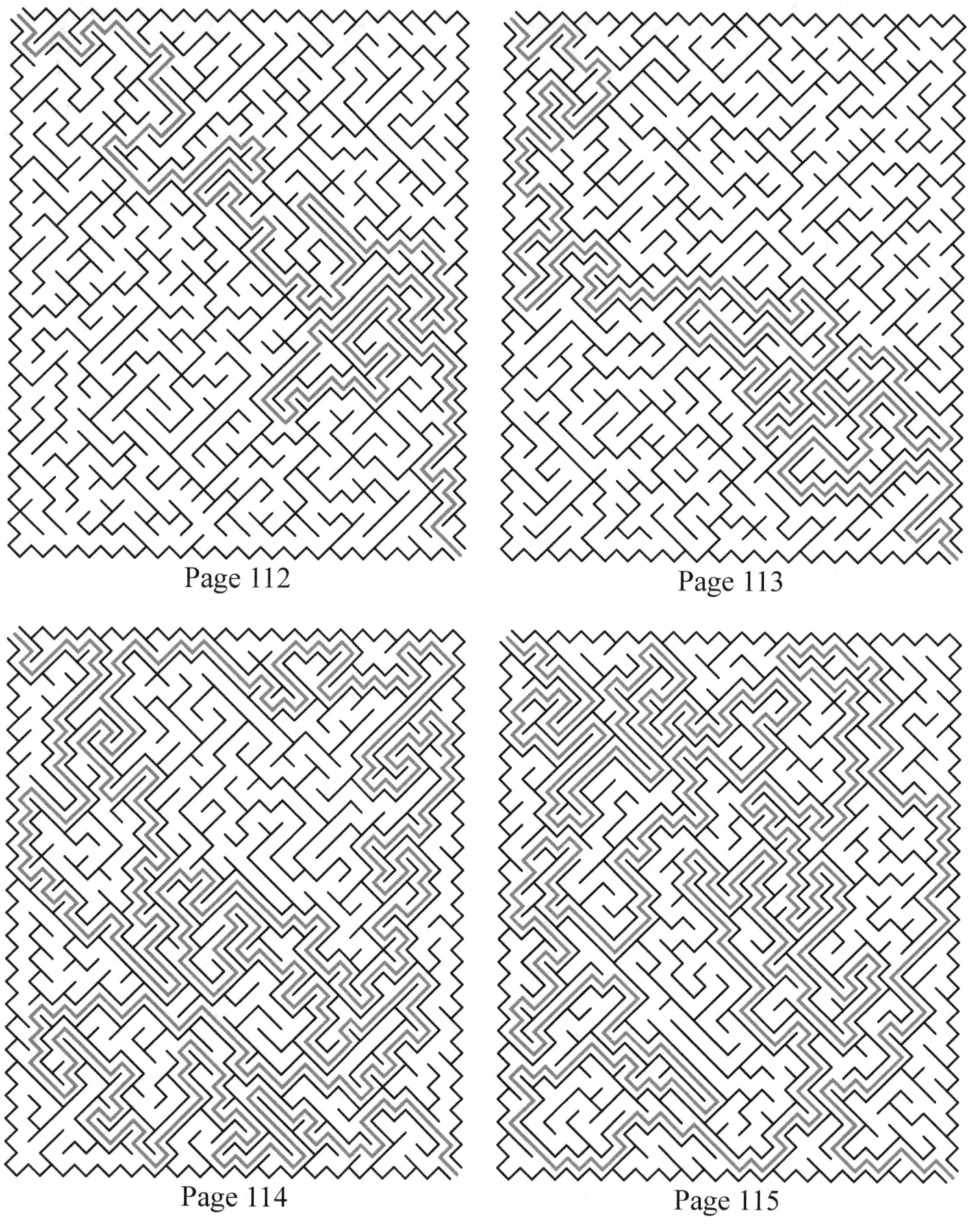

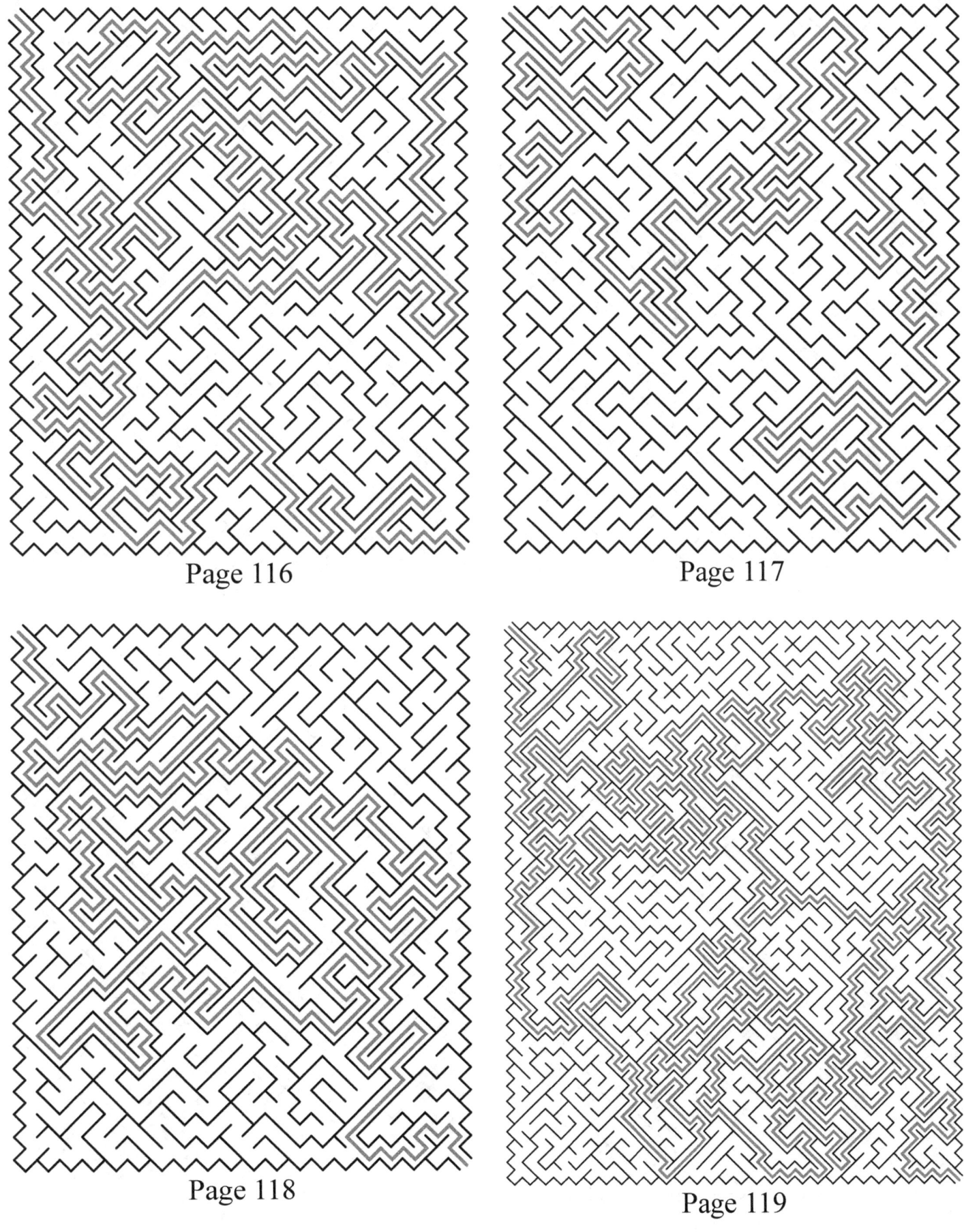

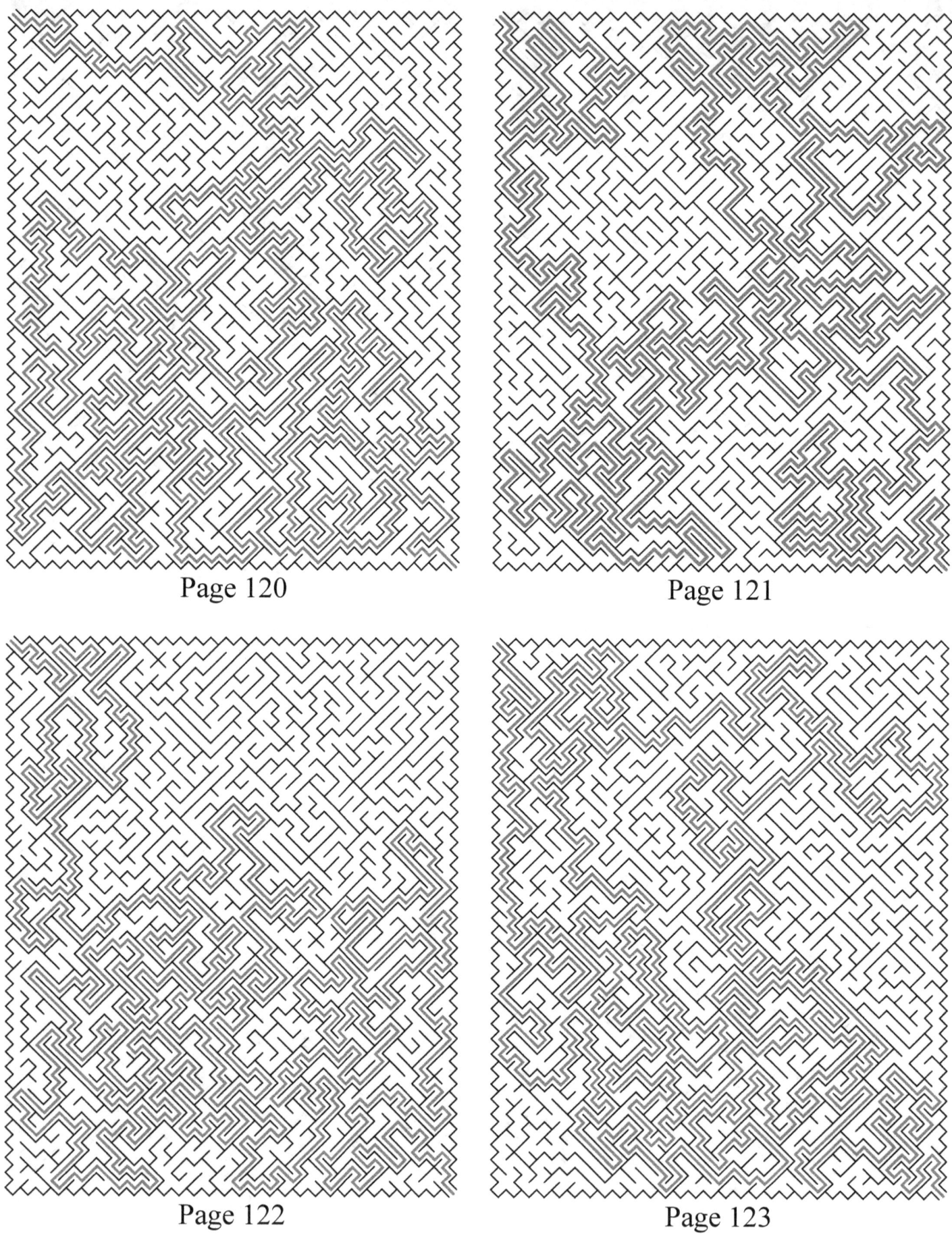

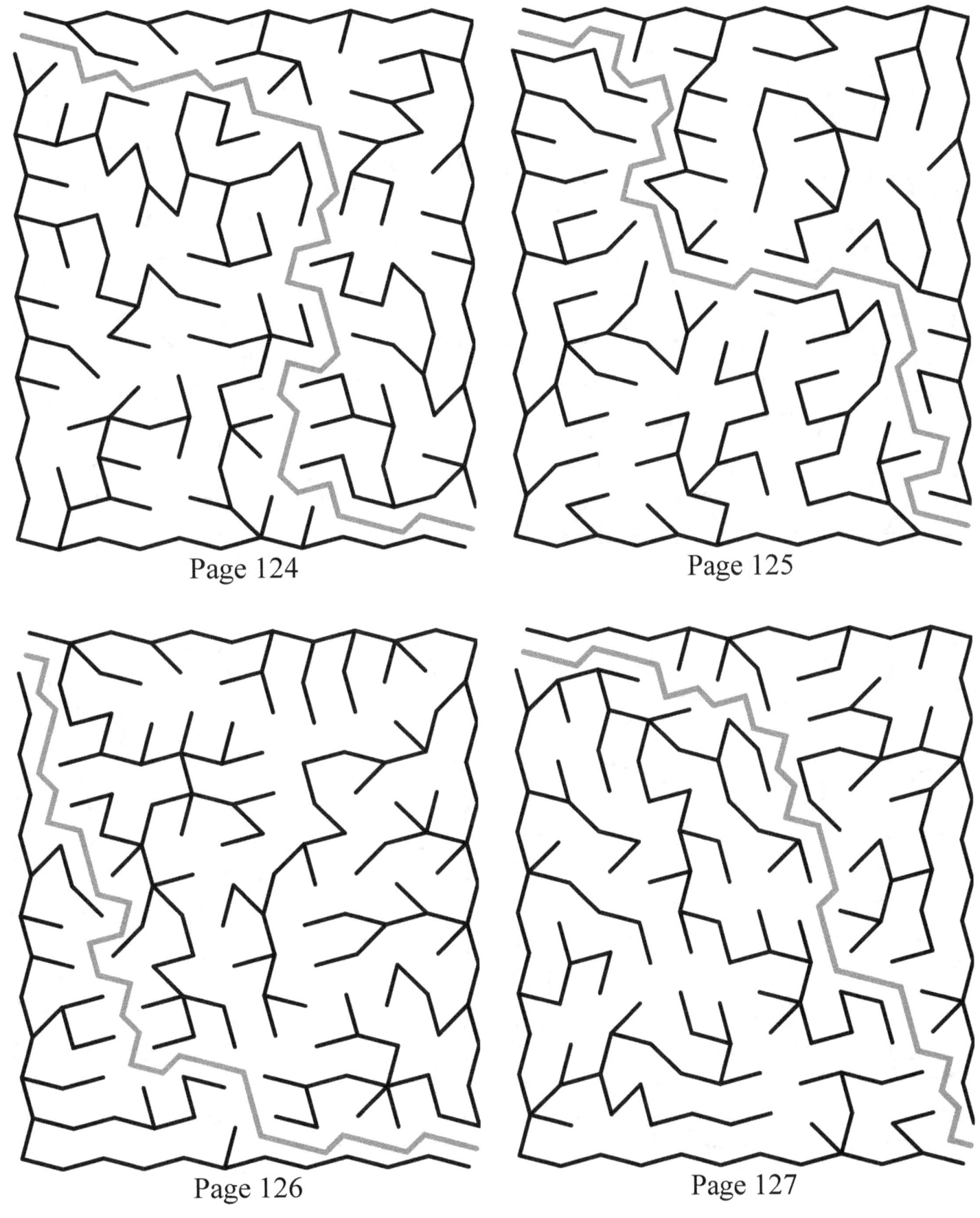

Page 124

Page 125

Page 126

Page 127

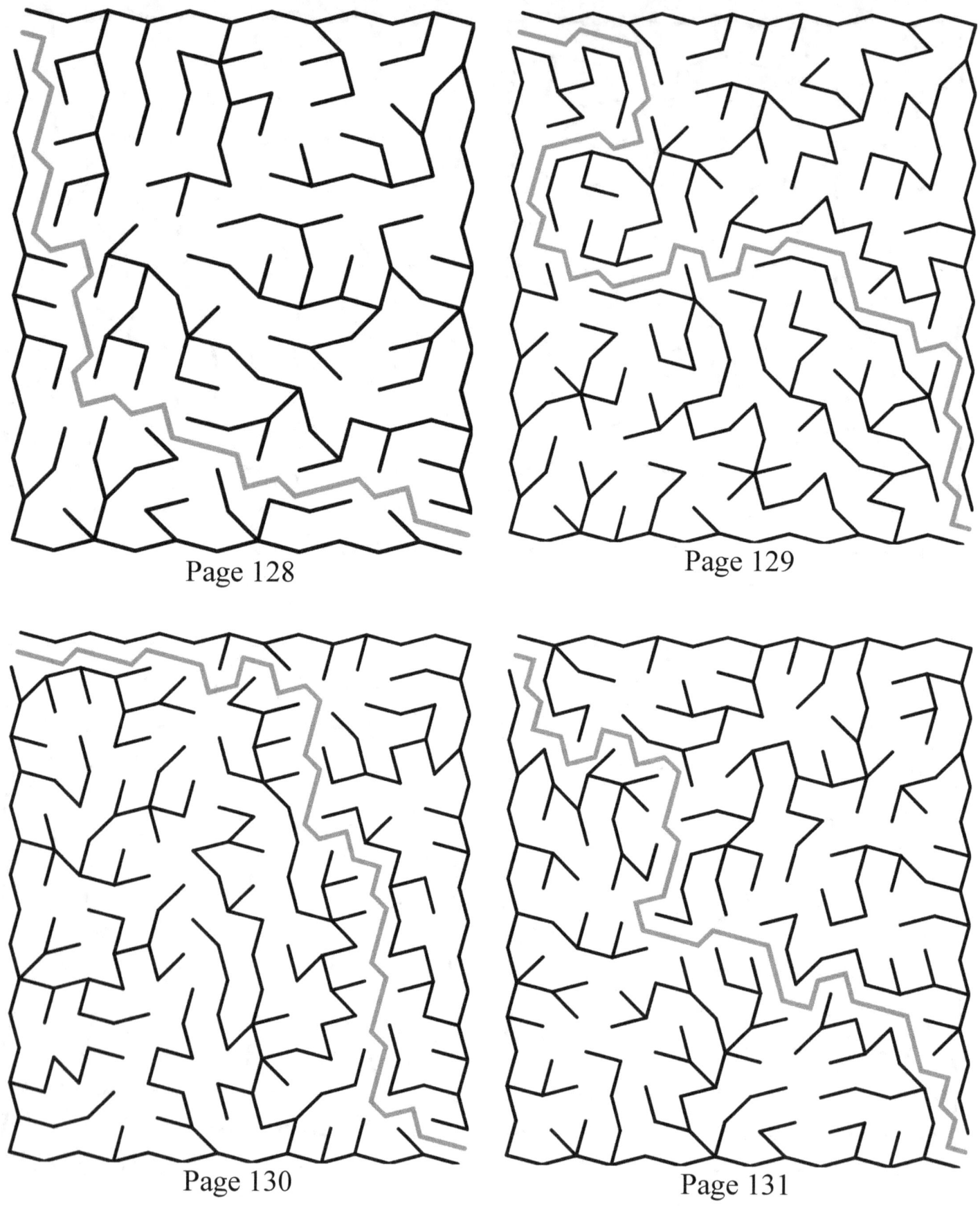

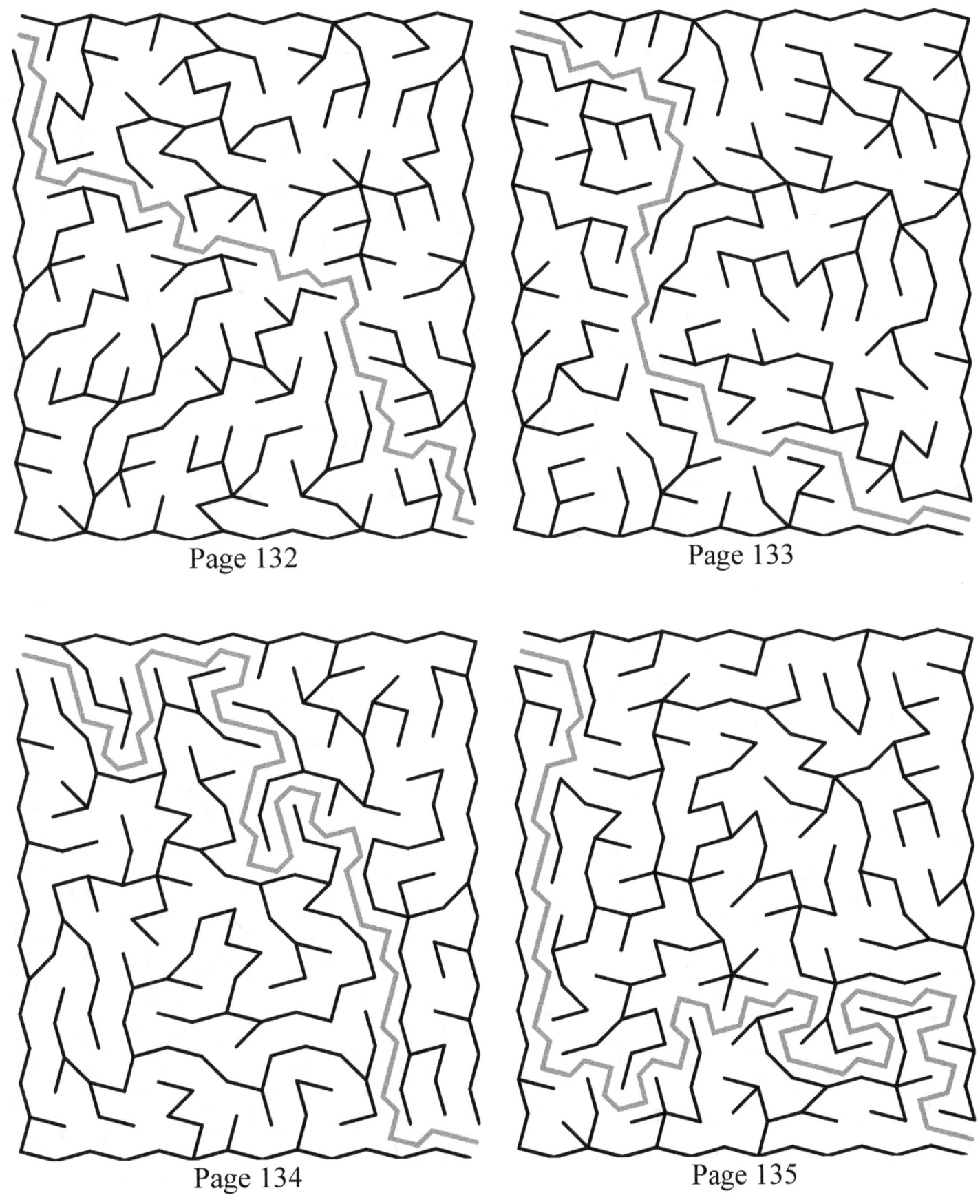

Page 132 Page 133

Page 134 Page 135

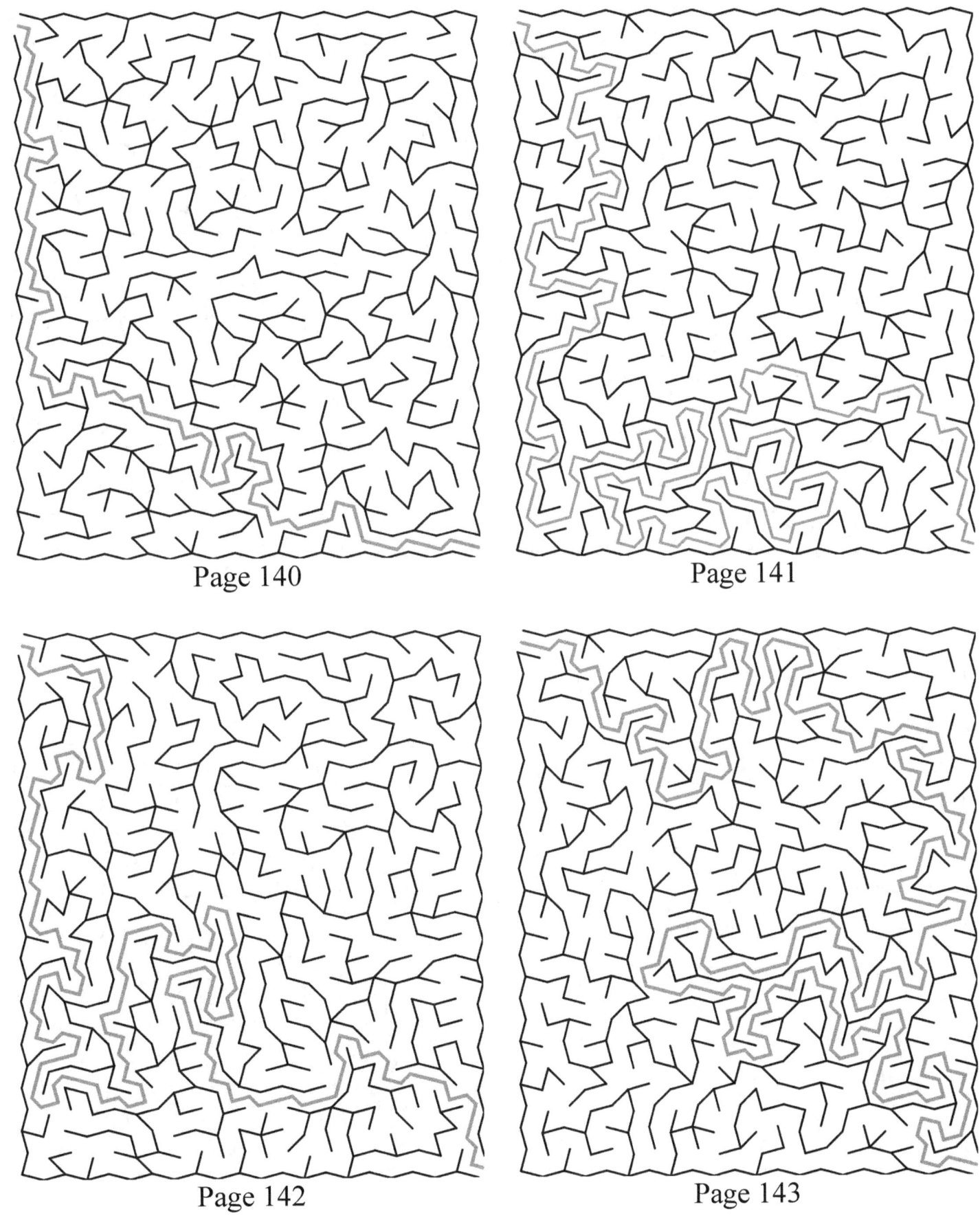

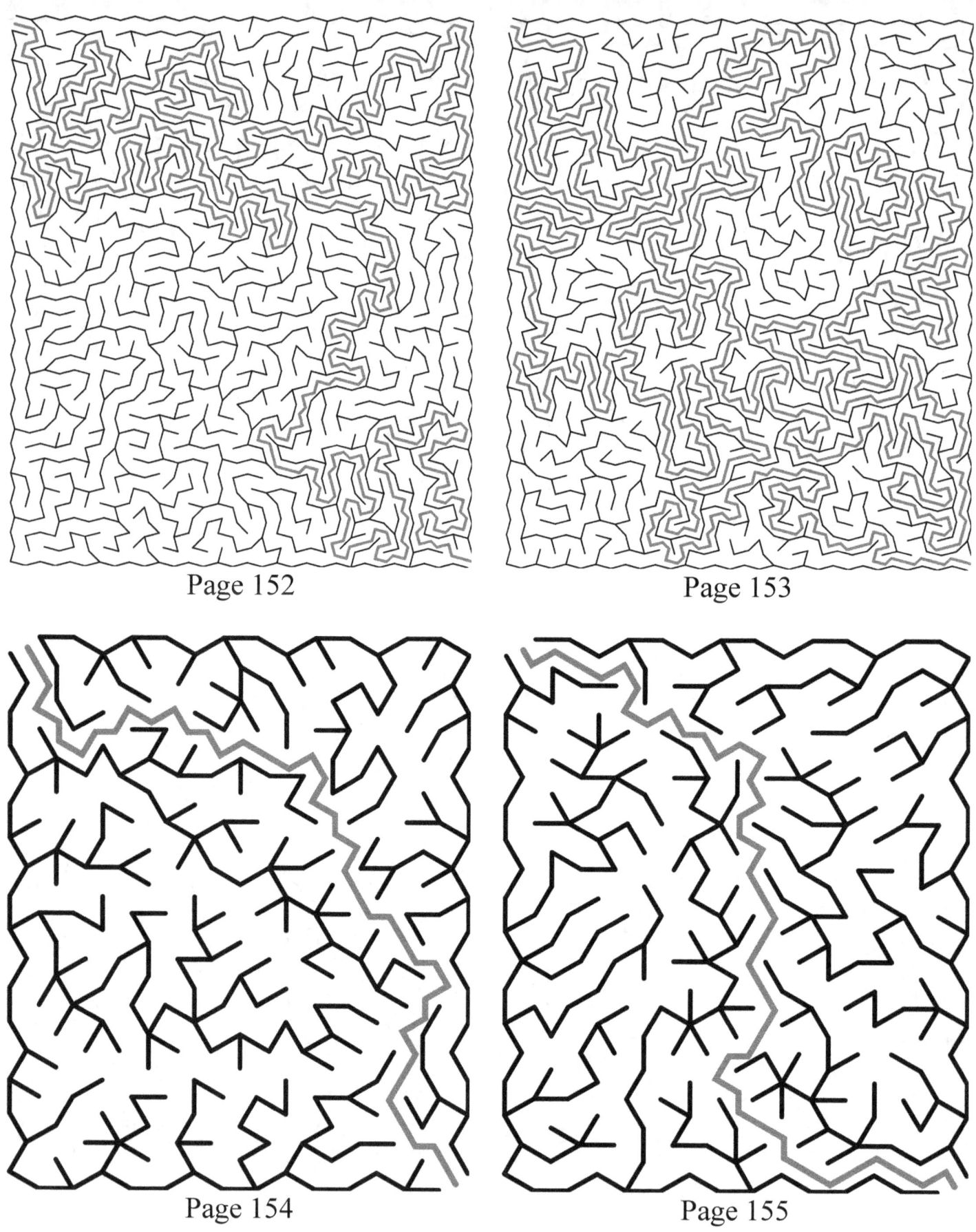

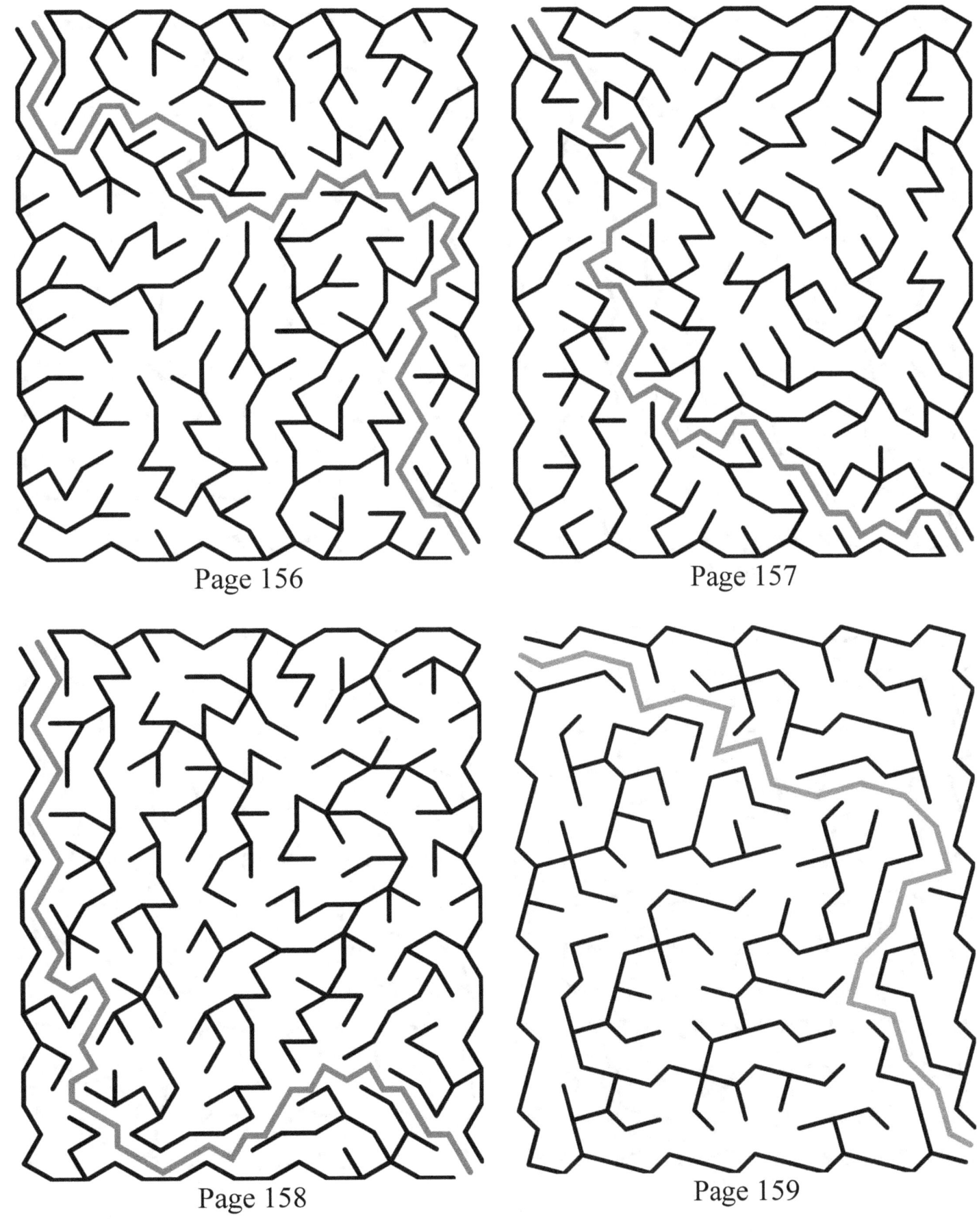

Page 156

Page 157

Page 158

Page 159

Page 160

Page 161

Page 162

Page 163

Page 164

Page 165

Page 166

Page 167

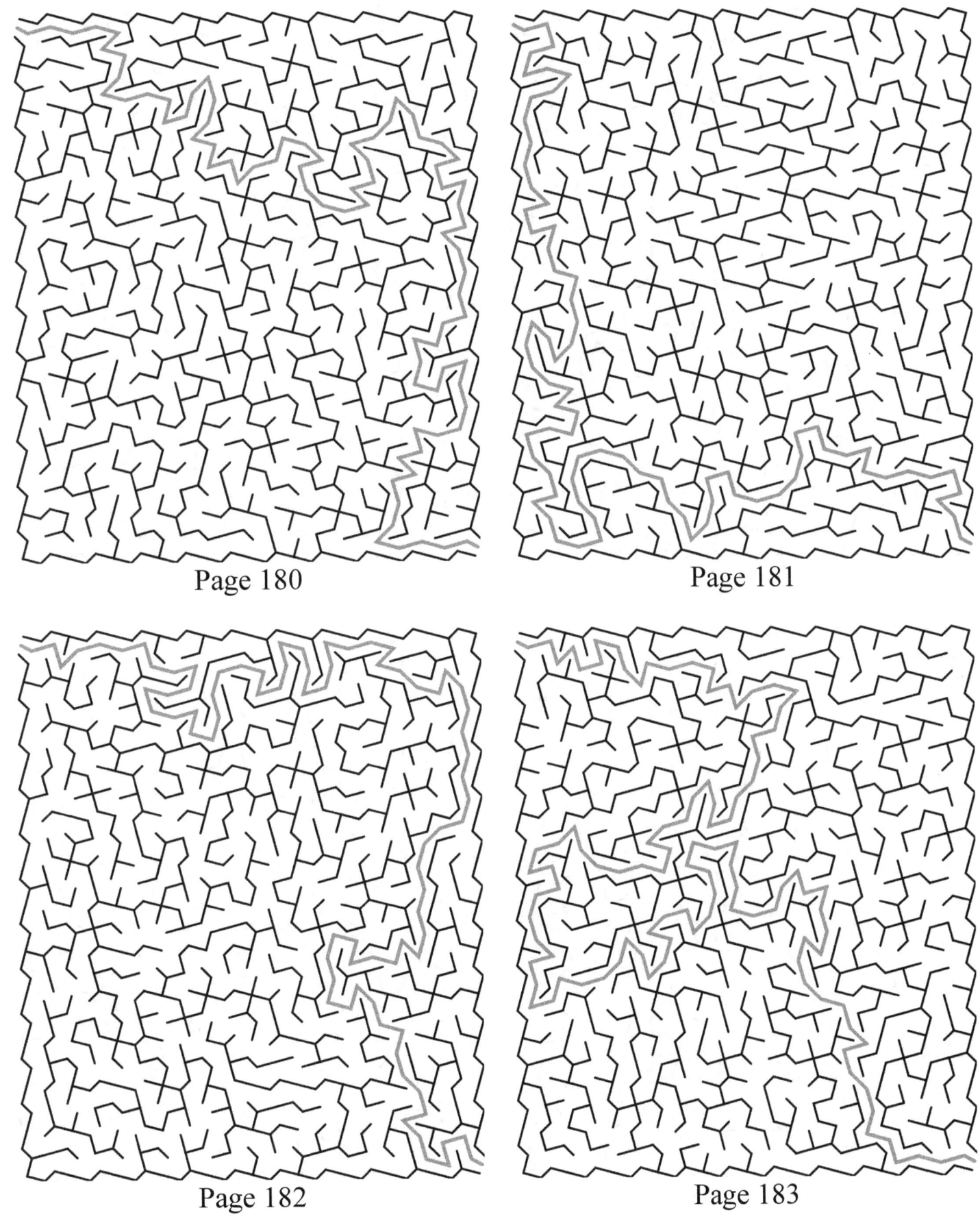

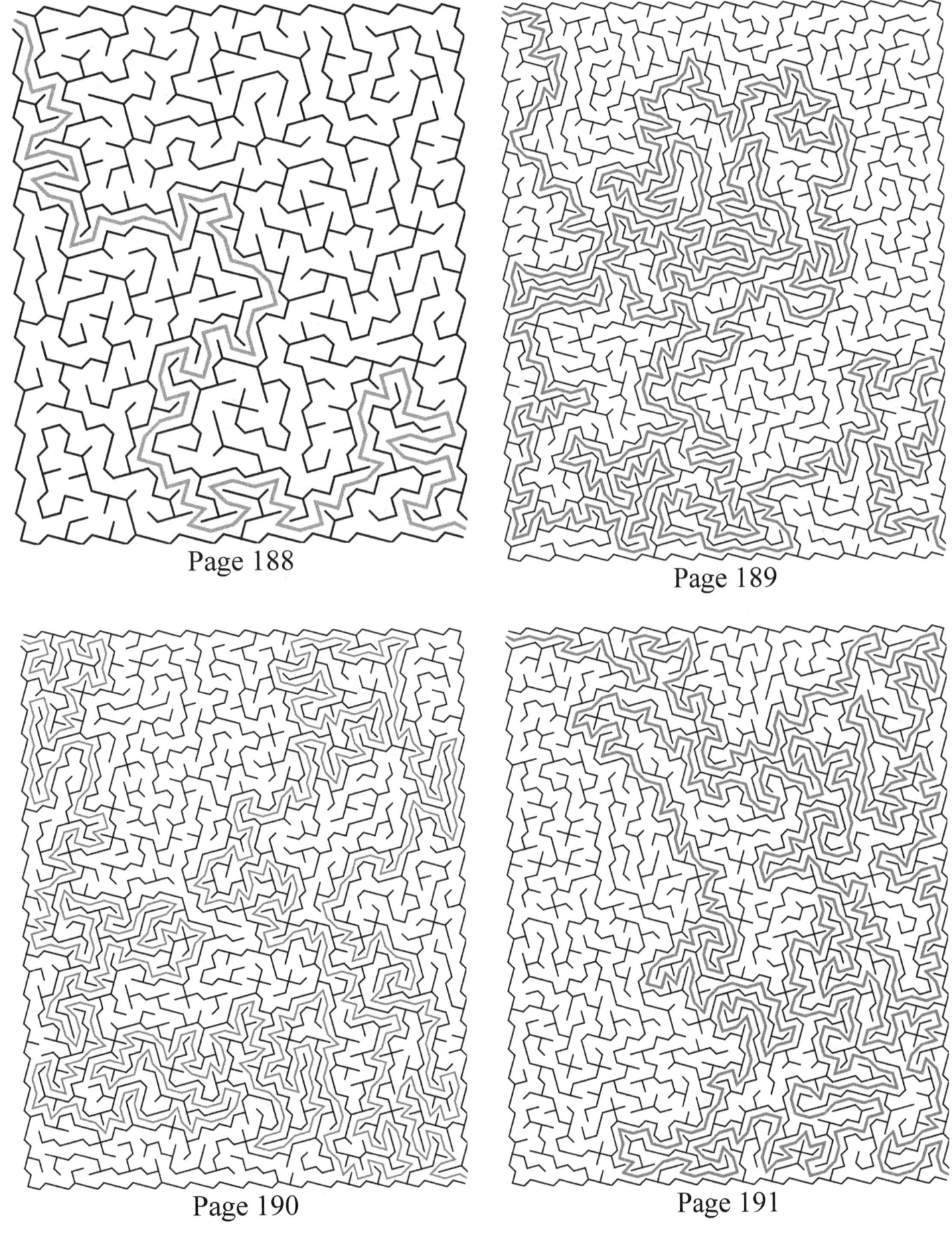

Page 188

Page 189

Page 190

Page 191

Page 192

Page 193

Page 194

Page 195

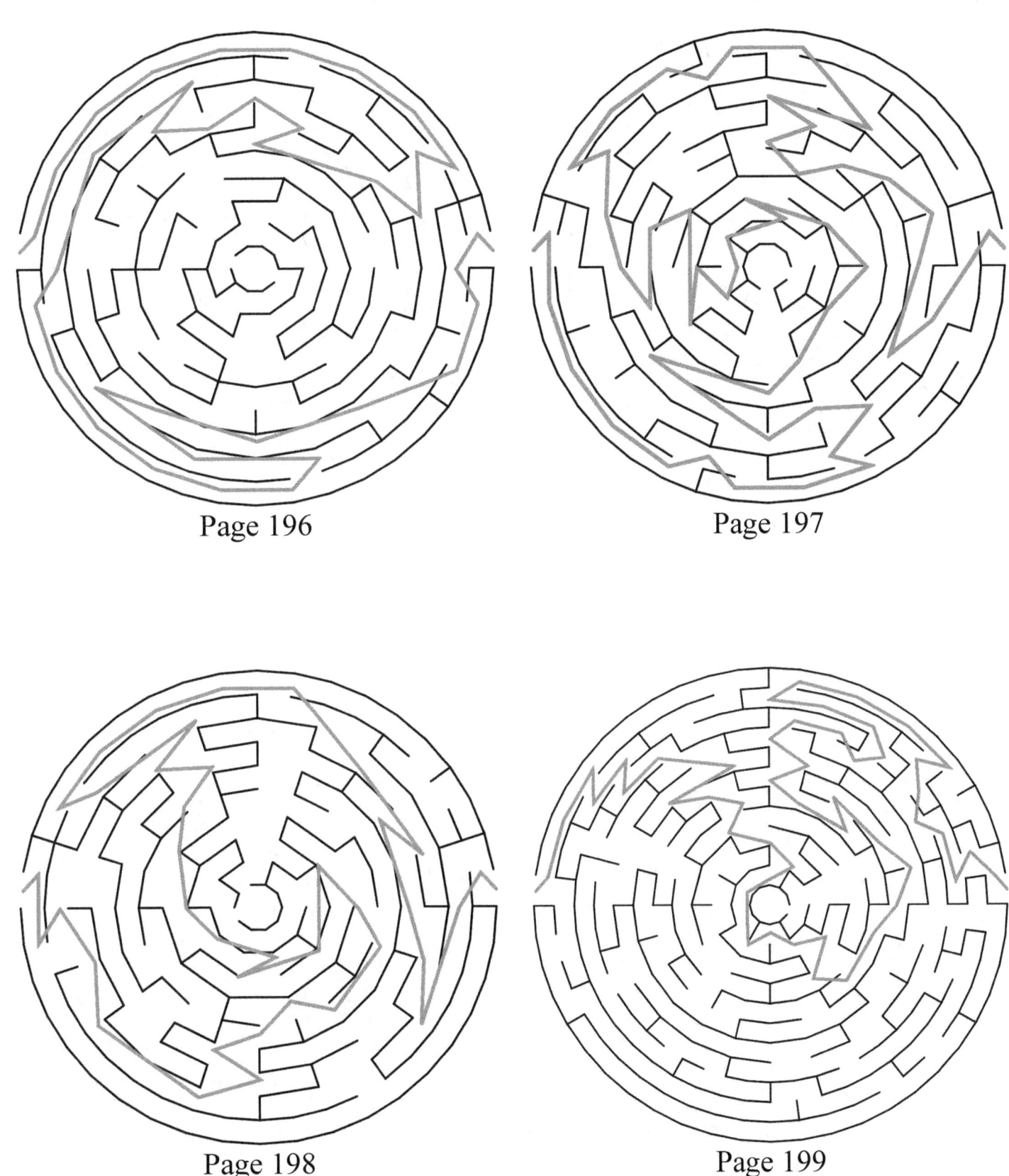

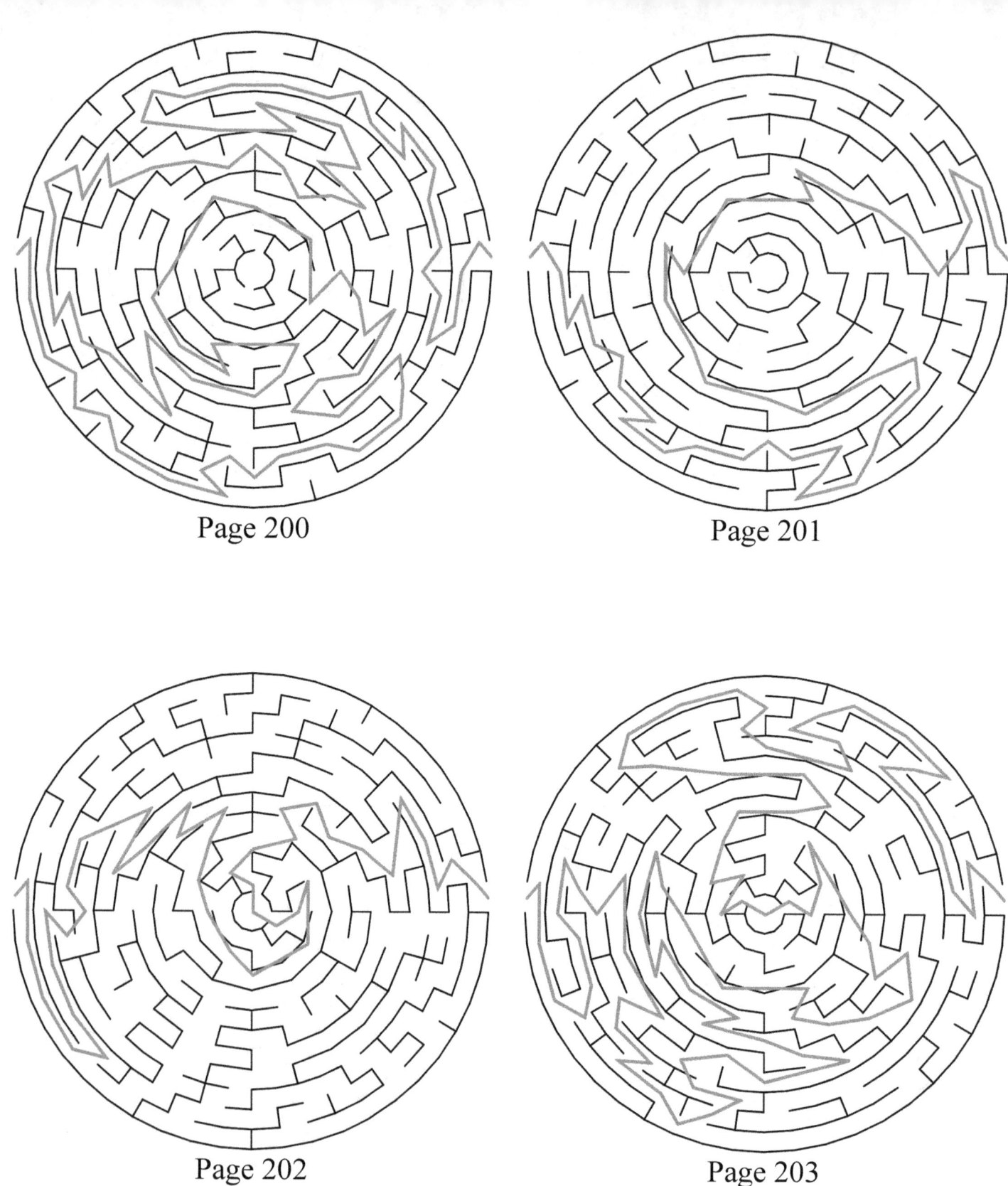

Page 200

Page 201

Page 202

Page 203

Page 204

Page 205

Page 206

Page 207

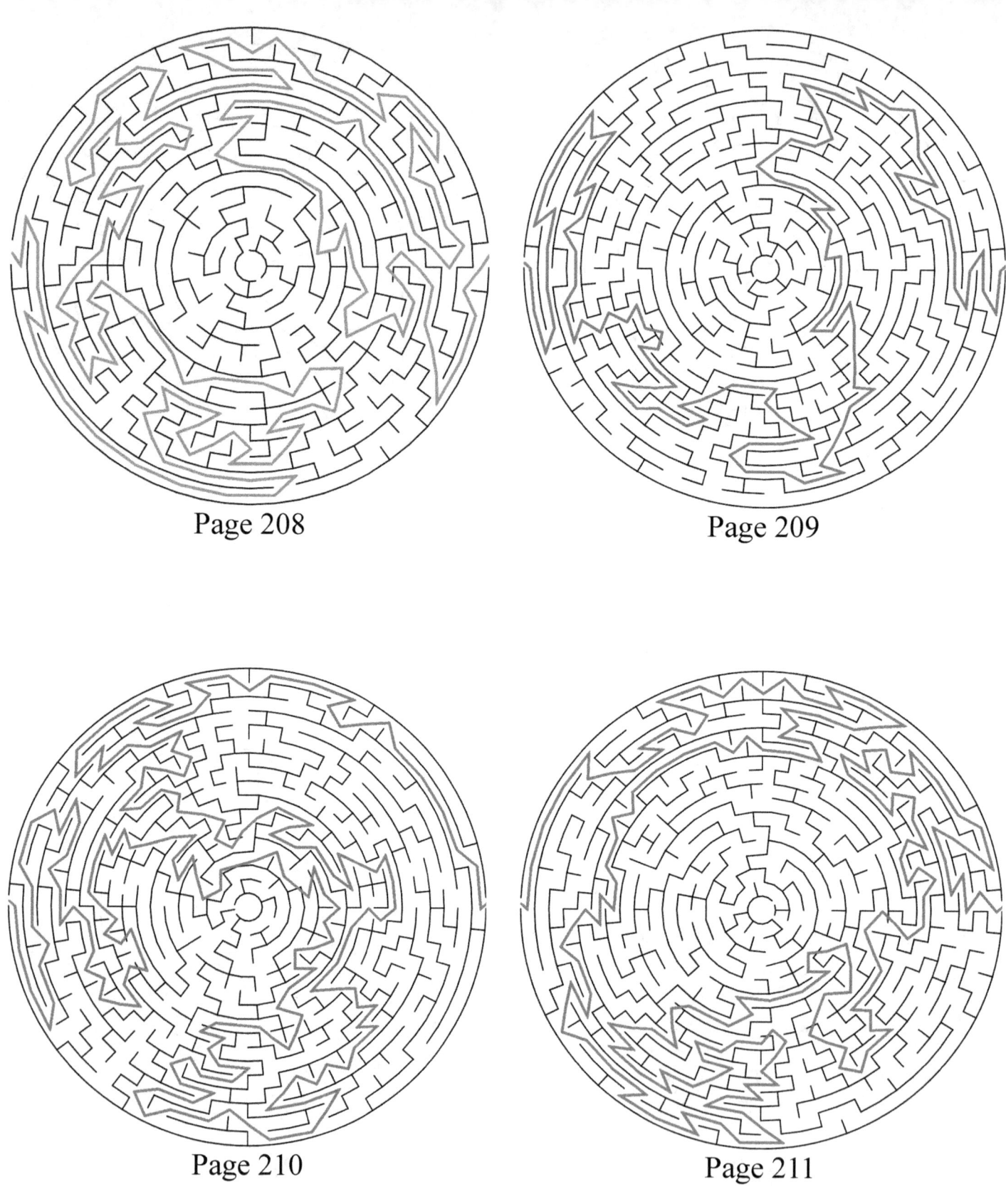

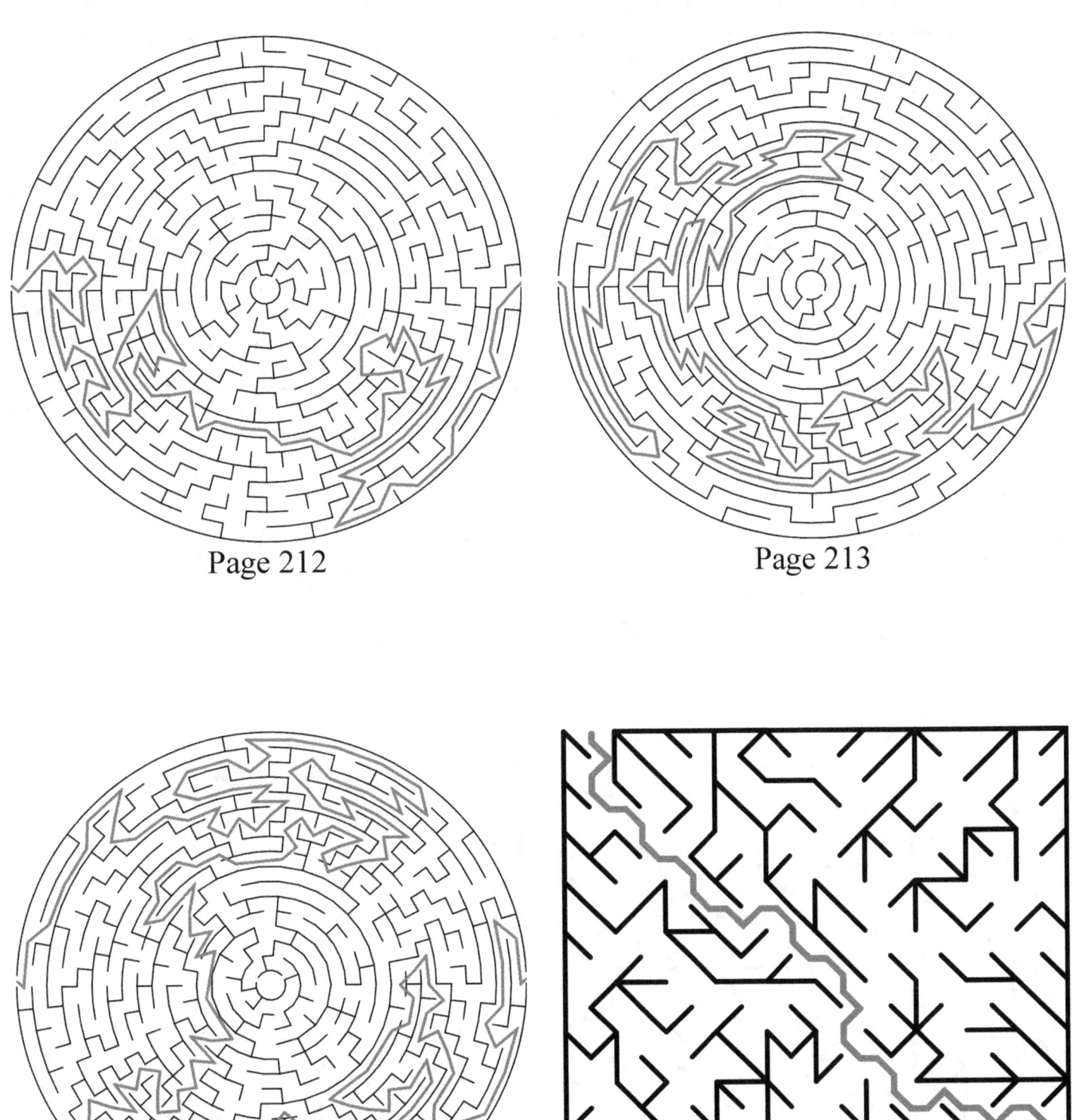

Page 212

Page 213

Page 214

Page 215

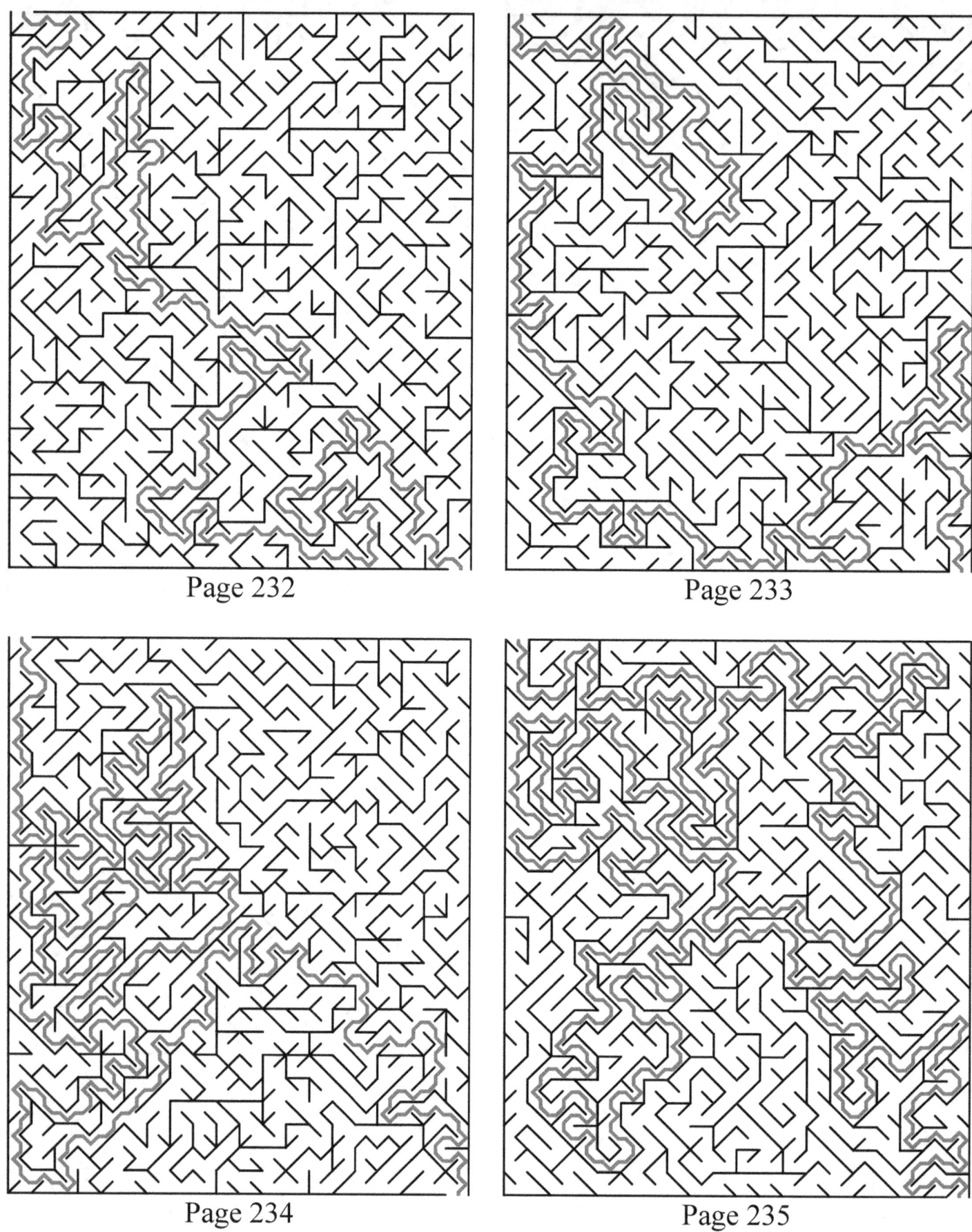

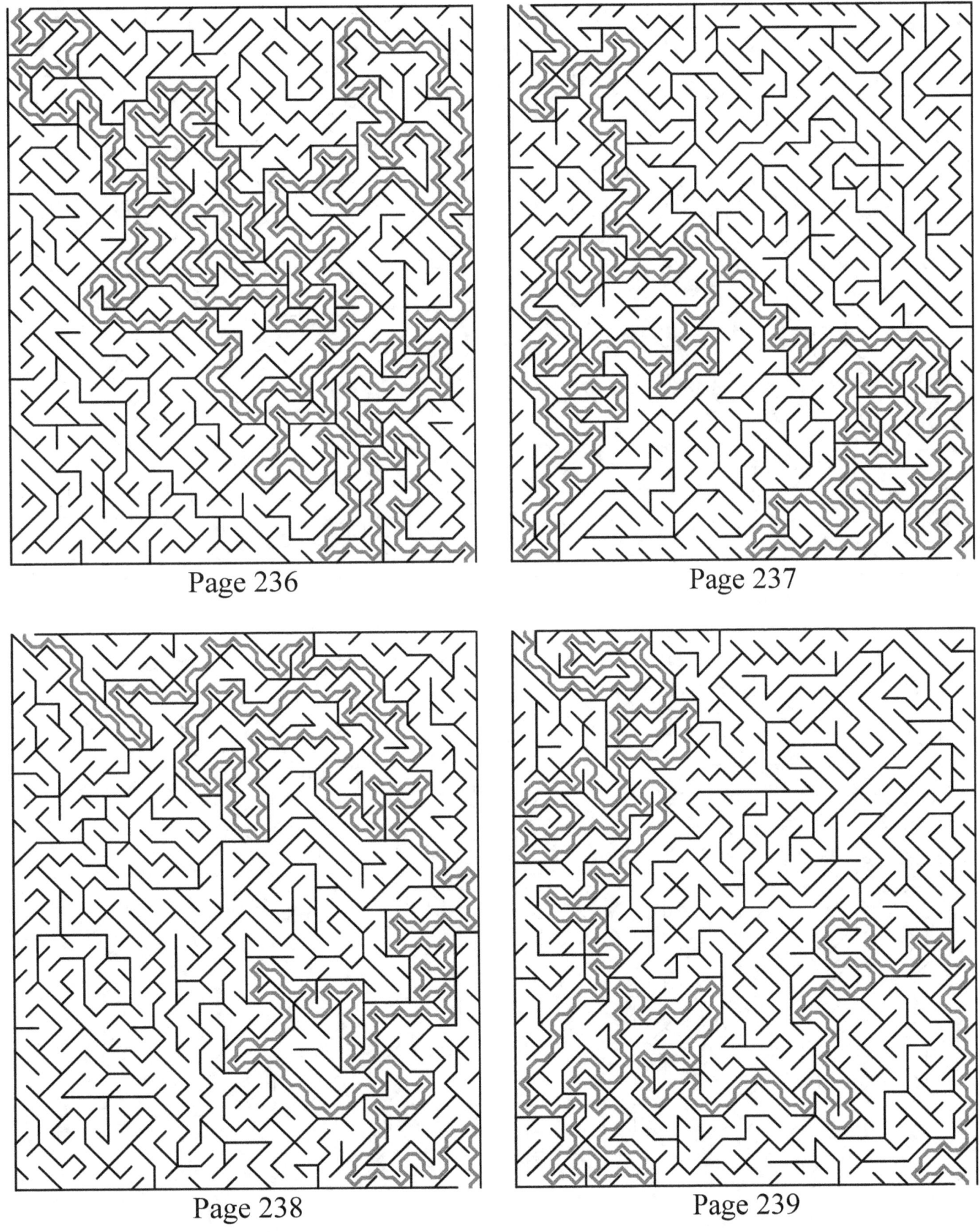

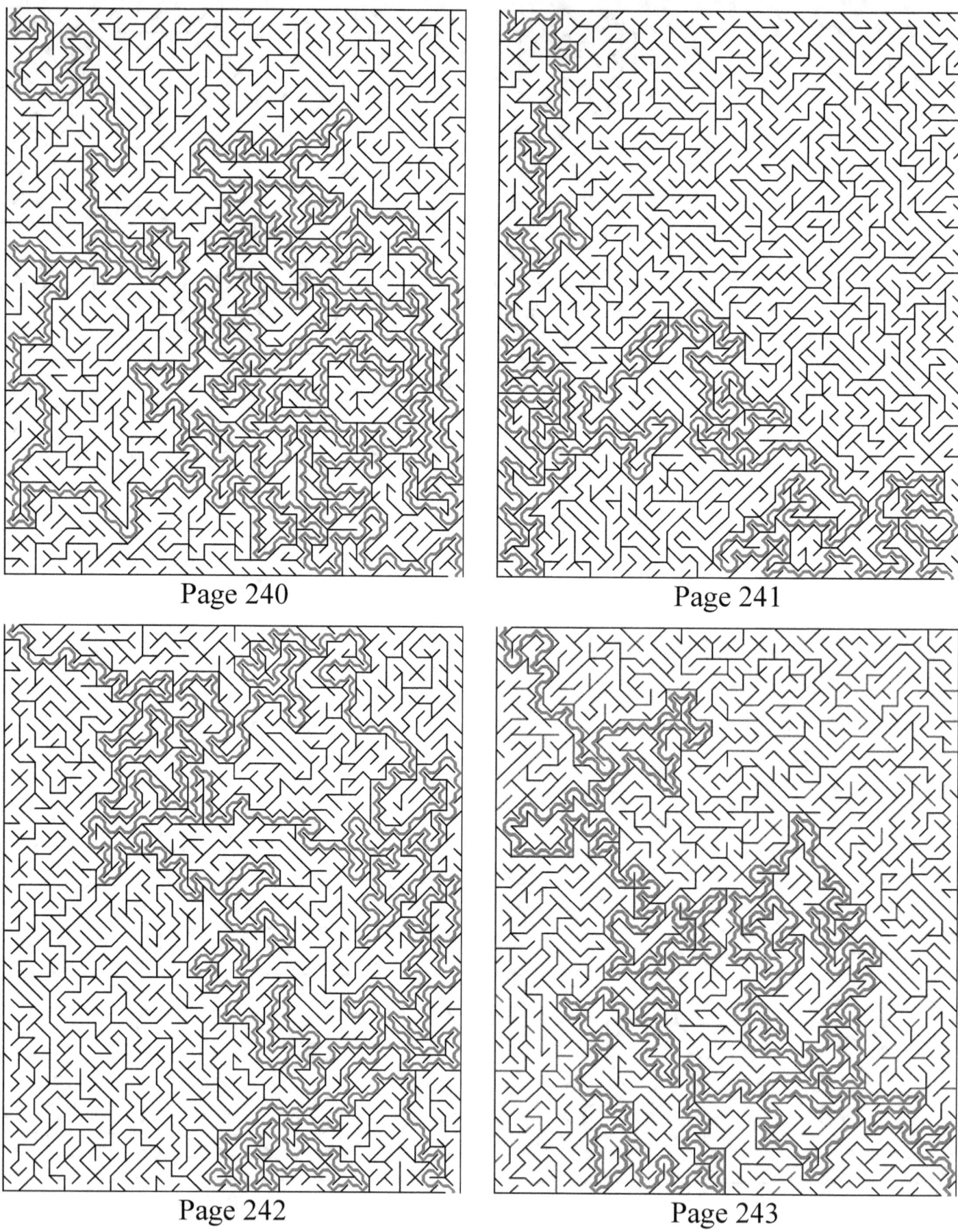

Page 240

Page 241

Page 242

Page 243

Page 244

Title Page

www.ingramcontent.com/pod-product-compliance
Lightning Source LLC
Chambersburg PA
CBHW081440070526
44586CB00019B/2182